*Teachings on Love*

# Teachings on Love

Thich Nhat Hanh

Parallax Press
Berkeley, California

Parallax Press
P.O. Box 7355
Berkeley, California 94707
www.parallax.org

Parallax Press is the publishing division of Unified Buddhist Church, Inc.

Cover design by Gay Reineck.
Author photograph by Dana Gluckstein.
Text design by Legacy Media, Inc.
Portions of the text were translated from Vietnamese by Mobi
Warren and Annabel Laity.
Edited by Arnie Kotler.

*Library of Congress Cataloging-in-Publication Data*

Nhât Hanh, Thích.
   Teachings on love/by Thich Nhat Hanh.
     p. cm.
   Translation of: Thuong Yêu Theo Phuong Pháp But Day
   "Translated from the Vietnamese by Mobi Warren and
Annabel Laity."—T.p. verso.
   ISBN 1-888375-12-4 (pbk)
    1. Love—Religious aspects—Buddhism.  2. Compassion
   (Buddhism).  3. Religious Life—Buddhism.  4. Buddhism—
   Doctrines.  I. Title.
BQ4360.N43  1997                                  97-153
294.3'5—dc21                                      CIP

6  7  8  9  10  /  08  07  06  05  04

# Contents

CHAPTER ONE

# *The Four Immeasurable Minds*

HAPPINESS IS ONLY POSSIBLE WITH TRUE LOVE. TRUE LOVE HAS the power to heal and transform the situation around us and bring a deep meaning to our lives. There are people who understand the nature of true love and how to generate and nurture it. The teachings on love given by the Buddha are clear, scientific, and applicable. Every one of us can benefit from these teachings.

During the lifetime of the Buddha, those of the Brahmanic faith prayed that after death they would go to Heaven to dwell eternally with Brahma, the universal God. One day a Brahman man asked the Buddha, "What can I do to be sure that I will be with Brahma after I die?" and the Buddha replied, "As Brahma is the source of Love, to dwell with him you must practice the *Brahmaviharas*—love, compassion, joy, and equanimity." A *vihara* is an abode or a dwelling place. Love in Sanskrit is *maitri;* in Pali it is *metta.* Compassion is *karuna* in both languages. Joy is *mudita.* Equanimity is *upeksha* in Sanskrit and *upekkha* in Pali. The Brahmaviharas are four elements of true love. They are called "immeasurable," because if you practice them, they will grow in you every day until they embrace the whole world. You will become happier, and everyone around you will become happier, also.

The Buddha respected people's desire to practice their own faith, so he answered the Brahman's question in a way that encouraged him to do so. If you enjoy sitting meditation, practice sitting meditation. If you enjoy walking meditation, practice walking meditation. But preserve your Jewish, Christian, or Muslim roots. That is the way to continue the Buddha's spirit. If you are cut off from your roots, you cannot be happy.

According to Nagarjuna, the second-century Buddhist philosopher:

> *Practicing the Immeasurable Mind of Love extinguishes anger in the hearts of living beings. Practicing the Immeasurable Mind of Compassion extinguishes all sorrows and anxieties in the hearts of living beings. Practicing the Immeasurable Mind of Joy extinguishes sadness and joylessness in the hearts of living beings. Practicing the Immeasurable Mind of Equanimity extinguishes hatred, aversion, and attachment in the hearts of living beings.*[1]

If we learn ways to practice love, compassion, joy, and equanimity, we will know how to heal the illnesses of anger, sorrow, insecurity, sadness, hatred, loneliness, and unhealthy attachments. In the *Anguttara Nikaya*, the Buddha teaches, "If a mind of anger arises, the *bhikkhu* (monk) can

---

[1] *Mahaprajñaparamita Shastra.* A shastra is a treatise or commentary on the Buddha's teachings, written by a great master after the lifetime of the Buddha. This text is available in Belgium as Nagarjuna, *Le Traité de La Grande Vertu de Sagesse,* translated by Étienne Lamotte (Louvain, Belgium: Institut Orientaliste, 1949).

practice the meditation on love, compassion, or equanimity for the person who has brought about the feeling of anger."[2]

Some sutra commentators have said that the Brahma-viharas are not the highest teaching of the Buddha, that they cannot put an end to suffering and afflictions. This is not correct. One time the Buddha said to his beloved attendant Ananda, "Teach these Four Immeasurable Minds to the young monks, and they will feel secure, strong, and joyful, without afflictions of body or mind. For the whole of their lives, they will be well equipped to practice the pure way of a monk."[3] On another occasion, a group of the Buddha's disciples visited the monastery of a nearby sect, and the monks there asked, "We have heard that your teacher Gautama teaches the Four Immeasurable Minds of love, compassion, joy, and equanimity. Our master teaches this also. What is the difference?" The Buddha's disciples did not know how to respond. When they returned to their monastery, the Buddha told them, "Whoever practices the Four Immeasurable Minds together with the Seven Factors of Enlightenment, the Four Noble Truths, and the Noble Eightfold Path will arrive deeply at enlightenment."[4] Love, compassion, joy, and equanimity are the very nature of an enlightened person. They are the four aspects of true love within ourselves and within everyone and everything.

---

[2] V, 161.

[3] *Madhyama Agama,* Sutra 86, *Taisho* 26.

[4] Sutra 744 of *Tsa A Han (Samyuktagama), Taisho* 99. Also *Mettasahagata Sutta, Samyutta Nikaya,* Vol. V, p. 115. For an explication of the Four Noble Truths and the Eightfold Path, see Thich Nhat Hanh, *The Heart of the Buddha's Teaching* (Berkeley: Parallax Press, 1997).

## LOVE (MAITRI)

The first aspect of true love is maitri, the intention and capacity to offer joy and happiness. To develop that capacity, we have to practice looking and listening deeply so that we know what to do and what not to do to make others happy. If you offer your beloved something she does not need, that is not maitri. You have to see her real situation or what you offer might bring her unhappiness.

In Southeast Asia, many people are extremely fond of a large, thorny fruit called durian. You could even say they are addicted to it. Its smell is extremely strong, and when some people finish eating the fruit, they put the skin under their bed so they can continue to smell it. To me, the smell of durian is horrible. One day when I was practicing chanting in my temple in Vietnam, there was a durian on the altar that had been offered to the Buddha. I was trying to recite the *Lotus Sutra,* using a wooden drum and a large bowl-shaped bell for accompaniment, but I could not concentrate at all. I finally carried the bell to the altar and turned it upside down to imprison the durian, so I could chant the sutra. After I finished, I bowed to the Buddha and liberated the durian. If you were to say to me, "Thây, I love you so much I would like you to eat some of this durian," I would suffer. You love me, you want me to be happy, but you force me to eat durian. That is an example of love without understanding. Your intention is good, but you don't have the correct understanding.

Without understanding, your love is not true love. You must look deeply in order to see and understand the needs, aspirations, and suffering of the one you love. We all need love. Love brings us joy and well-being. It is as natural as the air. We are loved by the air; we need fresh air to be happy and well. We are loved by trees. We need trees to be healthy. In order to be loved, we have to love, which means we have to understand. For our love to continue, we have to take the appropriate action or non-action to protect the air, the trees, and our beloved.

Maitri can be translated as "love" or "loving kindness." Some Buddhist teachers prefer "loving kindness," as they find the word "love" too dangerous. But I prefer the word "love." Words sometimes get sick and we have to heal them. We have been using the word "love" to mean appetite or desire, as in "I love hamburgers." We have to use language more carefully. "Love" is a beautiful word; we have to restore its meaning. The word "maitri" has roots in the word *mitra* which means friend. In Buddhism, the primary meaning of love is friendship.

We all have the seeds of love in us. We can develop this wonderful source of energy, nurturing the unconditional love that does not expect anything in return. When we understand someone deeply, even someone who has done us harm, we cannot resist loving him or her. Shakyamuni Buddha declared that the Buddha of the next eon will be named "Maitreya, the Buddha of Love."

## COMPASSION (KARUNA)

The second aspect of true love is karuna, the intention and capacity to relieve and transform suffering and lighten sorrows. Karuna is usually translated as "compassion," but that is not exactly correct. "Compassion" is composed of *com* ("together with") and *passion* ("to suffer"). But we do not need to suffer to remove suffering from another person. Doctors, for instance, can relieve their patients' suffering without experiencing the same disease in themselves. If we suffer too much, we may be crushed and unable to help. Still, until we find a better word, let us use "compassion" to translate karuna.

To develop compassion in ourselves, we need to practice mindful breathing, deep listening, and deep looking. The *Lotus Sutra* describes Avalokiteshvara as the bodhisattva who practices "looking with the eyes of compassion and listening deeply to the cries of the world." Compassion contains deep concern. You know the other person is suffering, so you sit close to her. You look and listen deeply to her to be able to touch her pain. You are in deep communication, deep communion with her, and that alone brings some relief.

One compassionate word, action, or thought can reduce another person's suffering and bring him joy. One word can give comfort and confidence, destroy doubt, help someone avoid a mistake, reconcile a conflict, or open the door to liberation. One action can save a person's life or help him take advantage of a rare opportunity. One thought can do the same, because thoughts always lead to words and actions. With compassion in our heart, every thought, word, and deed can bring about a miracle.

When I was a novice, I could not understand why, if the world is filled with suffering, the Buddha has such a beautiful smile. Why isn't he disturbed by all the suffering? Later I discovered that the Buddha has enough understanding, calm, and strength; that is why the suffering does not overwhelm him. He is able to smile to suffering because he knows how to take care of it and to help transform it. We need to be aware of the suffering, but retain our clarity, calmness, and strength so we can help transform the situation. The ocean of tears cannot drown us if karuna is there. That is why the Buddha's smile is possible.

## JOY (MUDITA)

The third element of true love is mudita, joy. True love always brings joy to ourselves and to the one we love. If our love does not bring joy to both of us, it is not true love.

Commentators explain that happiness relates to both body and mind, whereas joy relates primarily to mind. This example is often given: Someone traveling in the desert sees a stream of cool water and experiences joy. On drinking the water, he experiences happiness. *Ditthadhamma sukhavihari* means "dwelling happily in the present moment." We don't rush to the future; we know that everything is here in the present moment. Many small things can bring us tremendous joy, such as the awareness that we have eyes in good condition. We just have to open our eyes and we can see the blue sky, the violet flowers, the children, the trees, and so many other kinds of forms and colors. Dwelling in mindfulness, we can touch these wondrous and refreshing things, and our mind of joy arises naturally. Joy contains happiness and happiness contains joy.

Some commentators have said that mudita means "sympathetic joy" or "altruistic joy," the happiness we feel when others are happy. But that is too limited. It discriminates between self and others. A deeper definition of mudita is a joy that is filled with peace and contentment. We rejoice when we see others happy, but we rejoice in our own well-being as well. How can we feel joy for another person when we do not feel joy for ourselves? Joy is for everyone.

## EQUANIMITY (UPEKSHA)

The fourth element of true love is upeksha, which means equanimity, nonattachment, nondiscrimination, even-mindedness, or letting go. *Upa* means "over," and *iksh* means "to look." You climb the mountain to be able to look over the whole situation, not bound by one side or the other. If your love has attachment, discrimination, prejudice, or clinging in it, it is not true love. People who do not understand Buddhism sometimes think upeksha means indifference, but true equanimity is neither cold nor indifferent. If you have more than one child, they are all your children. Upeksha does not mean that you don't love. You love in a way that all your children receive your love, without discrimination.

Upeksha has the mark called *samatajñana,* "the wisdom of equality," the ability to see everyone as equal, not discriminating between ourselves and others. In a conflict, even though we are deeply concerned, we remain impartial, able to love and to understand both sides. We shed all discrimination and prejudice, and remove all boundaries between ourselves and others. As long as we see ourselves as the one who loves and the other as the one who is loved, as long as we value ourselves more than others or see ourselves as different from others, we do not have true equanimity. We have to put ourselves "into the other person's skin" and become one with him if we want to understand and truly love him. When that happens, there is no "self" and no "other."

Without upeksha, your love may become possessive. A summer breeze can be very refreshing; but if we try to put it in a tin can so we can have it entirely for ourselves, the breeze will die. Our beloved is the same. He is like a cloud, a breeze, a flower. If you imprison him in a tin can, he will die. Yet many people do just that. They rob their loved one of his liberty, until he can no longer be himself. They live to satisfy themselves and use their loved one to help them fulfill that. That is not loving; it is destroying. You say you love him, but if you do not understand his aspirations, his needs, his difficulties, he is in a prison called love. True love allows you to preserve your freedom and the freedom of your beloved. That is upeksha.

⚬

For love to be true love, it must contain compassion, joy, and equanimity. For compassion to be true compassion, it has to have love, joy, and equanimity in it. True joy has to contain love, compassion, and equanimity. And true equanimity has to have love, compassion, and joy in it. This is the interbeing nature of the Four Immeasurable Minds. When the Buddha told the Brahman man to practice the Four Immeasurable Minds, he was offering all of us a very important teaching. But we must look deeply and practice them for ourselves to bring these four aspects of love into our own lives and into the lives of those we love.

# CHAPTER TWO

# Love Meditation

THE BUDDHA OFFERED MANY MEDITATIONS ON LOVE. WHEN A group of monks told him that the spirits living near their forest monastery were causing others to suffer, the Buddha taught the *Metta Sutta (Discourse on Love):*

> *He or she who wants to attain peace should practice being upright, humble, and capable of using loving speech. He or she will know how to live simply and happily, with senses calmed, without being covetous and carried away by the emotions of the majority. Let him or her not do anything that will be disapproved of by the wise ones. [And this is what he or she contemplates]:*

> *"May everyone be happy and safe, and may their hearts be filled with joy.*

> *"May all living beings live in security and peace, beings who are frail or strong, tall or short, big or small, visible or not visible, near or far away, already born or yet to be born. May all of them dwell in perfect tranquility.*

*"Let no one do harm to anyone. Let no one put the life of anyone in danger. Let no one, out of anger or ill will, wish anyone any harm.*

*"Just as a mother loves and protects her only child at the risk of her own life, we should cultivate boundless love to offer to all living beings in the entire cosmos. Let our boundless love pervade the whole universe, above, below, and across. Our love will know no obstacles, our heart will be absolutely free from hatred and enmity. Whether standing or walking, sitting or lying, as long as we are awake, we should maintain this mindfulness of love in our own heart. This is the noblest way of living.*

*"Free from wrong views, greed, and sensual desires, living in beauty and realizing perfect understanding, those who practice boundless love will certainly transcend birth and death."*

After several months of reciting and practicing the *Metta Sutta*, the monks came to understand the sufferings of the troubled spirits. As a result, the spirits began to practice, also. They became filled with the energy of love, and the whole forest was peaceful.[1]

᾿

The Buddha also offered many specific exercises to help his disciples practice and realize the Four Immeasurable Minds:

---

[1] *Sutta Nipata*, Vol. I, Sutra 8.

*When your mind is filled with love, send it in one direction, then a second, a third, and a fourth, then above, and then below. Identify with everything, without hatred, resentment, anger, or enmity. This mind of love is very wide. It grows immeasurably and eventually is able to embrace the whole world. Practice the same way with your mind filled with compassion, then joy, then equanimity.[2]*

*With his mind filled with love, the monk permeates one direction, and then a second, a third, a fourth, above, below, and all around, everywhere identifying himself with all. He permeates the whole world with his mind filled with love, wide, far, developed, unbound, free from hatred and ill-will. He does the same with his mind filled with compassion, joy, and equanimity.[3]*

When the energy of love is strong in us, we can send it to beings in all directions. But we must not think that love meditation is only an act of imagination—we imagine our love as being like waves of sound or light, or like a pure, white cloud that forms slowly and gradually spreads out to envelop the whole world. A true cloud produces rain. Sound and light penetrate everywhere, and our love must do the same. We have to observe whether our mind of love is present in our actual contact with others. Practicing love meditation in the sitting position is only the beginning.

---

[2] *Madhyama Agama,* Sutra 86.

[3] *Subha Sutta, Majjhima Nikaya,* Sutra 99.

But it is an important beginning. We sit quietly and look deeply into ourselves. With practice, our love will increase naturally, becoming all-inclusive and all-embracing. As we learn to see with the eyes of love, we empty our mind of anger and hatred. As long as these negative mental formations are present in us, our love is incomplete. We may think we understand and accept others, but we are not yet able to love them fully. Nagarjuna says, "At the time you practice the Immeasurable Mind of Love, you must look deeply in order to face your anger and hatred."[4]

In the introduction to Nagarjuna's *Mahaprajñaparamita Shastra,* Étienne Lamotte, the translator, wrote, "The Four Immeasurable Minds are just platonic ideals," mere ideas, not something that can be realized. Although Professor Lamotte was an excellent translator, he was not actually familiar with Buddhist practice. The moment we give rise to the desire for all beings to be happy and at peace, the energy of love arises in our mind, and all our feelings, perceptions, mental formations, and consciousness are permeated by love; in fact, they *become* love. This is no mere "ideal." Nagarjuna addresses this directly:

> *When we want beings in all directions to be happy, there arises in us the intention to love. This desire to love enters our feelings, perceptions, mental formations, and consciousness; and it becomes manifested in all our actions, speech, and other mental activities. Events that are neither mental nor physical arising after that are in accord with love and can in them-*

---

[4] Lamotte, trans., *Le Traité de la Grande Vertu de Sagesse de Nagarjuna (Mahaprajñaparamita Shastra)* (see chap 1, n. 1).

*selves be called love, as love is their root. These events determine our future actions, and they are directed by our will, which is now suffused with love. Will is the energy that drives our actions and speech. The same is true with regard to the arising of compassion, joy, and equanimity.[5]*

Mindfulness is the energy that allows us to look deeply at our body, feelings, perceptions, mental formations, and consciousness and see clearly what our real needs are, so we will not drown in the sea of suffering. Eventually love fills our mind and our will, and all our actions from that time on manifest love. Speech and actions are the fruits of will, so when our will is permeated by love, our speech and actions are also suffused with love. We speak only loving and constructive words and act only in ways that bring happiness and relieve suffering.

Yet in another passage of the *Mahaprajñaparamita Shastra,* Nagarjuna also says that the Four Immeasurable Minds are mere aspirations, that they exist only in our mind. This is much the same as Professor Lamotte's platonic ideals. It was Nagarjuna who provided the words for Lamotte! It helps us understand if we remember that Nagarjuna wanted to advance the views of the newly emerg-

---

[5] *Mahaprajñaparamita Shastra.* According to the Buddha, a human being is composed of five *skandhas* (elements, heaps, or aggregates): form, feelings, perceptions, mental formations, and consciousness. For a full explanation of practicing love meditation within each of the five skandhas, see Chapter Three. "Events" that are considered neither mental nor physical are related to our mind and objects of our mind. They are listed as gain, loss, birth, death, grammar, literature, time, space, union, separation, impermanence, quantity, seeing things as similar or dissimilar, etc. Will, volition, or intention is *chetana.*

ing Mahayana Buddhism, so he wrote, "Followers of Hinayana practice the Four Immeasurable Minds, but the Immeasurable Minds they practice are only in the form of aspirations. The Immeasurable Minds, when joined with the *paramitas* of the Mahayana,[6] are the Immeasurable Minds of the bodhisattva that can transform the world." In his efforts to promote the Mahayana, Nagarjuna erred in saying that the Four Immeasurable Minds of the Hinayana are merely internal, without external manifestation. This contradicts his previous words, that when the mind of love arises, it manifests in our words and our actions. To say that love, compassion, joy, and equanimity are only aspirations that exist in the mind is not correct. We practice not only to give rise to the Four Immeasurables in our mind, but also to bring them into the world through our words and actions. When we practice love meditation, we don't merely visualize our love spreading into space. We touch the deep sources of love that are already in us, and then, in the midst of our daily lives, in our actual contact with others, we express and share our love. We practice until we see the concrete effects of our love on others, until we are able to offer peace and happiness to everyone, even those who have acted toward us in ways that are most unlovable.

Buddhaghosa, author of *The Path of Purification (Visuddhimagga)*[7], tells us that when our meditation begins

---

[6] *The Ten Paramitas* of the Mahayana are: *dana* (generosity), *shila* (precepts), *kshanti* (forbearance), *virya* (energy), *dhyana* (meditation), *prajña* (understanding), *upaya* (skillful means), *pranidhana* (aspiration), *bala* (spiritual power), and *jñana* (wisdom).

[7] Bhikkhu Nanamoli, trans., *The Path of Purification: Visuddhi Magga, The Classic Manual of Buddhist Doctrine & Meditation* (Kandy: Buddhist Publication Society, 1975).

to bear fruit, we will recognize in ourselves these signs of a loving mind: (1) our sleep is more relaxed, (2) we do not have nightmares, (3) our waking state is more at ease, (4) we are not anxious or depressed, and (5) we are loved and protected by everyone and everything around us.

In the *Anguttara Nikaya,* the Buddha mentions eleven advantages of practicing love meditation. The Buddha speaks in these terms—of what is advantageous and what is disadvantageous—because doing so encourages people to practice.

1. The practitioner sleeps well.
2. Upon waking, he or she feels well and light in his heart.
3. He does not have unpleasant dreams.
4. She is well-liked by many people. She feels at ease with everyone. Others, especially children, like to be near her.
5. He is dear to the nonhuman species: birds, fish, elephants, squirrels. Species that are visible and invisible like to be near him.
6. She is supported and protected by gods and goddesses.
7. He is protected from fire, poison, and the sword. He does not need to make any special effort to avoid them.
8. She reaches meditative concentration easily.
9. His face is bright and clear.
10. At the time of death, her mind is clear.
11. He is reborn in the Brahma Heaven, where he can continue the practice, because there is already a Sangha of those practicing the Four Immeasurable Minds.[8]

---

[8] *Metta Sutta, Anguttara Nikaya, Ekadasaka Nipata* ("Chapter on Eleven Things"), Sutta 16 (Vol. V, p. 342).

In the *Itivuttaka*, the Buddha says if we gather together all the virtuous actions we have realized in this world, they are not equal to practicing love meditation. Building practice centers, making Buddha figures, casting bells, or doing social work cannot bring about one-sixteenth of the merit of practicing love meditation. If we collect together all the light from the stars, it will not be as bright as the light of the moon. In the same way, practicing love meditation is greater than all other virtuous actions combined.[9]

Practicing love meditation is like digging deep into the ground until we reach the purest water. We look deeply into ourselves until insight arises and our love flows to the surface. Joy and happiness radiate from our eyes, and everyone around us benefits from our smile and our presence.

When practitioners of Mahayana Buddhism say, "Hinayana Buddhists don't take care of other people, they only take care of themselves, they are on a lesser vehicle," they do not realize that if you take good care of yourself, you help everyone. You stop being a source of suffering to the world, and you become a reservoir of joy and freshness. Here and there are people who know how to take good care of themselves, who live joyfully and happily. They are our strongest support. Everything they do, they do for everyone. That is the meaning of Mahayana Buddhism. That is love meditation.

The Buddha said that if a monk practices love meditation even if only for the length of time it takes to snap one's fingers, that monk is worthy of being a monk: "He will not

---

[9] *Mettabhavana Sutta, Itivuttaka,* Sutta 27 (p. 13).

fail in meditative concentration. He will realize the teachings given by teachers on the path. The food offered to him as alms will not be wasted. There is no greater virtue than practicing love meditation every day."[10]

[10] *Apara-Accharasanghatavaggo, Anguttara Nikaya, Ekaka Nipata* ("Chapter on One Thing"), Sutta 31 (Vol. I, p. 38).

CHAPTER THREE

# *Self-Love*

THIS IS A LOVE MEDITATION ADAPTED FROM THE *VISUDDHIMAGGA*:

*May I be peaceful, happy, and light in body and spirit.*
*May he/she be peaceful, happy, and light in body and spirit.*
*May they be peaceful, happy, and light in body and spirit.*

*May I be safe and free from injury.*
*May he/she be safe and free from injury.*
*May they be safe and free from injury.*

*May I be free from anger, afflictions, fear, and anxiety.*
*May he/she be free from anger, afflictions, fear, and anxiety.*
*May they be free from anger, afflictions, fear, and anxiety.*

We begin practicing this love meditation on ourselves ("I"). Until we are able to love and take care of ourselves, we cannot be of much help to others. After that we can practice on others ("he/she," "they")—first on someone we like, then on someone neutral to us, then someone we love, and finally someone the mere thought of whom makes us suffer.

We begin this practice by looking deeply into the *skandha* of form, which is our body. According to the Buddha, a human being is made of five skandhas (elements, heaps, or aggregates): form, feelings, perceptions, mental formations, and consciousness. We are the king, and these elements are our territory. To know the real situation within ourselves, we have to survey our own territory thoroughly, including the elements within us that are at war with each other. To bring about harmony, reconciliation, and healing within, we have to understand ourselves. Looking and listening deeply, surveying our territory, is the beginning of love meditation.

We begin by asking, How is my body in this moment? How was it in the past? How will it be in the future? Later, when we meditate on someone we like, someone neutral to us, someone we love, and someone we hate, we also begin by looking at her physical aspects. Breathing in and out, we visualize her face; her way of walking, sitting, and talking; her heart, lungs, kidneys, and all the organs in her body, taking as much time as we need to bring these details into awareness. But we always start with ourselves. When we see our own five skandhas clearly, understanding and love arise naturally, and we know what to do and what not to do to take better care of ourselves.

We look into our body to see whether it is at peace or suffering from illness. We look at the condition of our lungs, our heart, our intestines, our kidneys, and our liver to see what the real needs of our body are. When we do, we will eat, drink, and act in ways that demonstrate our love and our compassion for our body. Usually we just follow ingrained habits. But when we look deeply, we see that many of these habits harm our body and mind, so we work to transform our habits into ways conducive to good health and vitality.

Next we observe our feelings—whether they are pleasant, unpleasant, or neutral. Feelings flow in us like a river, and each feeling is a drop of water in that river. We look into the river of our feelings and see how each feeling came to be. We see what has been preventing us from being happy, and we do our best to transform those things. We practice touching the wondrous, refreshing, and healing elements that are already in us and in the world. Doing so, we become stronger and better able to love ourselves and others.

Then we meditate on our perceptions. The Buddha observed, "The person who suffers most in this world is the person who has many wrong perceptions.... And most of our perceptions are erroneous." We see a snake in the dark and we panic, but when our friend shines a light on it, we see that it is only a rope. We have to know which wrong perceptions cause us to suffer. Please calligraph the sentence, "Are you sure?" on a piece of paper and tape it to your wall. Love meditation helps us learn to look with clarity and serenity in order to improve the way we perceive.

Next we observe our mental formations, the ideas and tendencies within us that lead us to speak and act as we do. We practice looking deeply to discover the true nature of our mental formations—how we are influenced by our individual consciousness and also by the collective consciousness of our family, ancestors, and society. Unwholesome mental formations cause so much disturbance; wholesome mental formations bring about love, happiness, and liberation.

Finally we look at our consciousness. According to Buddhism, consciousness is like a field with every possible kind of seed in it—seeds of love, compassion, joy, and equanimity; seeds of anger, fear, and anxiety; and seeds of mindfulness. Consciousness is the storehouse that contains all these seeds, all the possibilities of what might arise in our mind. When our mind is not at peace, it may be because of the desires and feelings in our store consciousness. To live in peace, we have to be aware of our tendencies—our habit energies—so we can exercise some self-control. This is the practice of preventive health care. We look deeply into the nature of our feelings to find their roots, to see which feelings need to be transformed, and we nourish those feelings that bring about peace, joy, and well-being.

One day, King Prasenajit of Koshala asked Queen Mallika, "My dear wife, is there anyone who loves you as much as you love yourself?" The queen laughed and responded, "My dear husband, is there anyone who loves you more than you love yourself?" The next day, they told the Buddha of their conversation, and he said, "You are correct. There is no one in the universe more dear to us than ourselves. The mind may travel in a thousand directions, but it will find no one else more beloved. The moment you see how important it is to love yourself, you will stop making others suffer."[1]

King Prasenajit and the Buddha became close friends. One day, while they were sitting together in the Jeta Grove, the king said to the Buddha, "Master, there are people who think they love themselves, but who harm themselves all the time by their thoughts, words, and deeds. These people are their own worst enemy." The Buddha agreed, "Those who harm themselves through their thoughts, words, or actions are indeed their own worst enemies. They only

---

[1] *Mallika Sutta, Samyutta Nikaya,* Vol. I, p. 75.

bring themselves suffering."[2] We usually think our suffering is caused by others—our parents, our partner, our enemies. But out of forgetfulness, anger, or jealousy, we say or do things that create suffering for ourselves and others. Another time the Buddha told King Prasenajit, "People usually think they love themselves. But because they are not mindful, they say and do things that create their own suffering."[3] When we see that this is true, we will stop blaming others as the cause of our suffering. Instead, we will try to love and care for ourselves and nourish our own body and mind.

To practice this love meditation from the *Visuddhimagga,* sit still, calm your body and your breathing, and recite, "May I be peaceful, happy, and light in body and spirit. May I be safe and free from injury. May I be free from anger, afflictions, fear, and anxiety." The sitting position is a wonderful position for practicing this. Sitting still, we are not too preoccupied with other matters, so we can look deeply at ourselves as we are, cultivate our love for ourselves, and determine the best ways to express this love in the world.

The practice begins with an aspiration: "May I be...." Then we transcend the level of aspiration and look deeply at all the positive and negative characteristics of the object of our meditation, in this case ourselves. The willingness to love is not yet love. We look deeply, with all our being, in order to understand. We don't just repeat the words, or imitate others, or strive after some ideal. The practice of love meditation is not auto-suggestion. We don't just say, "I love myself. I love all beings." We look deeply at our body,

---

[2] *Piya Sutta, Samyutta Nikaya,* Vol. I, p. 71.

[3] *Piya Sutta, Samyutta Nikaya,* Vol. I, p. 71.

our feelings, our perceptions, our mental formations, and our consciousness, and in just a few weeks, our aspiration to love will become a deep intention. Love will enter our thoughts, our words, and our actions, and we will notice that we have become peaceful, happy, and light in body and spirit; safe and free from injury; and free from anger, afflictions, fear, and anxiety.

When you practice, observe how much peace, happiness, and lightness you already have. Notice whether you are anxious about accidents or misfortunes, and how much anger, irritation, fear, anxiety, or worry are already in you. As you become aware of the feelings in you, your self-understanding will deepen. You will see how your fears and lack of peace contribute to your unhappiness, and you will see the value of loving yourself and cultivating a heart of compassion. Instead of living with some generalized fear of accidents, observe the ways you injure yourself all the time, and take appropriate actions to minimize illness and injury.

Look deeply, not just while on your meditation cushion but wherever you are, whatever you are doing. Living mindfully is the best way to prevent accidents and protect yourself. Recognize your deep desire to live in peace and safety, to have the support you need, and to practice mindfulness. You might like to write down some of your observations and insights. The Buddha said that once we realize that we are the closest and most precious person on Earth to ourselves, we will stop treating ourselves as an enemy.[4] This practice dissolves in us any wish we might have to harm ourselves or others.

---

[4] *Mallika Sutta, Samyutta Nikaya,* Vol. I, p. 75.

"May I be free from anger, afflictions, fear, and anxiety." Anger is a hazard that affects everyone, including ourselves. When we are overcome by anger, our peace and happiness vanish. Some people's lives are consumed by anger. They become furious when someone just bumps into them. Is this because of the circumstances or because of the seeds of anger in them? Look deeply at the seeds of anger in yourself; look deeply at those you think have brought you harm. Love meditation helps us understand both, and it helps us let go of our habitual patterns of thought and action that create more suffering. We see that the person who has harmed us is himself suffering very much. Contemplating his suffering generates understanding and love in us, and with these energies, healing is possible. When our heart is opened, our suffering diminishes right away. The practice of love meditation liberates us from our afflictions.

A Brahman asked the Buddha, "Master, is there anything you would agree to kill?" and the Buddha answered, "Yes, anger. Killing anger removes suffering and brings peace and happiness. Anger is the single enemy that all the wise ones agree to kill." The Buddha's response impressed him, and he became a monk in the Buddha's Sangha. When the man's cousin learned that he had become a monk, he cursed the Buddha to his face. The Buddha only smiled. The man became even more incensed and asked, "Why don't you respond?" The Buddha replied, "If someone refuses a gift, it must be taken back by the one who offered it." Angry words and actions hurt, first of all, oneself.

After that, the Buddha recited this verse:

*For those with no anger,*
*how can anger arise?*

*When you practice deep looking and master yourself,*
*you dwell in peace, freedom, and safety.*
*The one who offends another*
*after being offended by him,*
*harms himself and harms the other.*
*When you feel hurt*
*but do not hurt the other,*
*you are truly victorious.*
*Your practice and your victory benefit both of you.*
*When you understand the roots of anger in yourself and in*
    *the other,*
*your mind will enjoy true peace, joy, and lightness.*
*You become the doctor who heals himself and heals the other.*
*If you don't understand,*
*you will think not getting angry to be the act of a fool.*[5]

"Those with no anger" means people who have no seeds of anger in their store consciousness. We get angry, first of all, because of the seeds of anger we carry within, seeds that may have been transmitted by our parents and our society. Even a small irritation can bring that anger to the surface. A person without seeds of anger can smile no matter what is said to him.

"When you practice deep looking and master yourself, you dwell in peace, freedom, and safety." People who are able to exercise self-control are not drawn into the cycle of anger. The insight they have gained through looking deeply protects their mind and body. Looking deeply is the practice of love, compassion, joy, and equanimity.

---

[5] *The Sutra of 42 Chapters, Taisho* 784.

"The one who offends another after being offended by him, harms himself and harms the other." When someone shouts at you, if you shout back, you suffer, the other person suffers, and the anger continues to escalate. Avoid such actions. They only harm both sides.

"When you feel hurt but do not hurt the other, you are truly victorious. Your practice and your victory benefit both of you." When you get hurt, hurting the other person will only cause the suffering to continue. Practice mindful breathing and you will create a win-win situation for both sides.

"When you understand the roots of anger in yourself and in the other, your mind will enjoy true peace, joy, and lightness." Looking deeply, you see that the other person is angry because of her lack of mindfulness, her wrong understanding, or the seeds of anger transmitted by her parents, ancestors, or society. This understanding will bring you peace, joy, and freedom right away.

"You become the doctor who heals himself and heals the other." When someone shouts at you angrily and you respond by smiling, without anger, that person may slowly begin to understand and eventually transform his anger. You heal your illness and that of others, like a great physician.

"If you don't understand, you will think not getting angry to be the act of a fool." They might say, "Fight back! Don't let yourself be talked to like that!" but they do not yet understand this deep teaching of the Buddha. When you feel anger arising, remember to return to your breathing and follow it. The other person may see that you are practicing, and she may even apologize. It can be beneficial to memorize this verse.

We pray that our daily lives will be free from hazards and injuries. We hope that anger will not arise. But if it does arise, we know how to deal with it. In this love meditation from the *Visuddhimagga,* "anger, afflictions, fear, and anxiety" refer to all the unwholesome, negative states of mind that dwell in us and rob us of our peace and happiness. Anger, fear, anxiety, craving, greed, and ignorance are the great afflictions of our time. By practicing mindful living, we are able to deal with them, and our love is translated into effective action.

Practice looking deeply all day long—during sitting meditation, walking meditation, at work, and at home. When you do, you will discover the true nature of the five skandhas—form, feelings, perceptions, mental formations, and consciousness. You will see the conditions that have caused you to be the way you are, and this makes it easy to accept yourself—your suffering and your happiness at the same time. To love is first of all to accept yourself as you actually are. "Knowing thyself" is the first practice of love.

# CHAPTER FOUR

# *Love and Understanding*

THESE THREE EXERCISES ARE A CONTINUATION OF THE LOVE
meditation based on the *Visuddhimagga:*

> *May I learn to look at myself with the eyes of understanding
> and love.*
> *May he/she learn to look at him/herself with the eyes of
> understanding and love.*
> *May they learn to look at themselves with the eyes of under-
> standing and love.*

> *May I be able to recognize and touch the seeds of joy and
> happiness in myself.*
> *May he/she be able to recognize and touch the seeds of joy
> and happiness in him/herself.*
> *May they be able to recognize and touch the seeds of joy and
> happiness in themselves.*

> *May I learn to identify and see the sources of anger, craving,
> and delusion in myself.*
> *May he/she learn to identify and see the sources of anger,
> craving, and delusion in him/herself.*
> *May they learn to identify and see the sources of anger,
> craving, and delusion in themselves.*

Last winter, when the residents of Plum Village practiced love meditation, one young laywoman said to me, "When I meditated on my boyfriend, I found that I began to love him less. And when I meditated on the person I dislike the most, I suddenly hated myself." Before the meditation, her love for her boyfriend was so passionate she was not able to see his shortcomings. During her practice, she began to see him more clearly, and she realized that he is less perfect than she had imagined. She said she loved him less, but in fact she began to love him in a way that has more maitri and karuna in it. She was able to recognize his suffering, and therefore her love deepened and became healthier. She was able to breathe more freely and to let him breathe more freely also. Although she said, "I love him less," I think she meant, "I love him more."

She also had fresh insights into the person she disliked the most. Suddenly she saw some of the reasons he was like that, and she saw how she had caused him to suffer by reacting so harshly to his words and actions. Her statement proved that she was really practicing.

"May I learn to look at myself with the eyes of understanding and love." Again, we begin with ourselves, to understand our own true nature. As long as we reject ourselves, as long as we continue to harm our own body and mind, there is no point in talking about loving and accepting others. With mindfulness, we will be able to recognize our habitual ways of thinking and the contents of our thoughts. Sometimes our thoughts run around in circles, and we are engulfed in distrust, pessimism, conflict, sorrow, or jealousy. When our mind is like that, our words and actions will naturally manifest these characteristics of mind and cause harm to ourselves and others. The practice is to shed the light of mindfulness on our habitual thought patterns so we can see them clearly. When a thought or idea arises, we recognize it and smile to it. That may be enough to make it cease. Appropriate mental attention *(yoniso manasikara)* brings us happiness, peace, clarity, and love. Inappropriate attention *(ayoniso manasikara)* fills our mind with sorrow, anger, and prejudice. Mindfulness helps us practice appropriate attention and water the seeds of peace, joy, and liberation in us.

In Buddhism, the mind *(manas)* is likened to a monkey swinging from branch to branch, leading us again and again into the dark world of pain and suffering. The practice is to shine the light of mindfulness on our mind's paths so we can see them clearly and prevent our mind from wandering down paths of inappropriate attention. Whenever we hear a conversation or witness an event, our attention can be appropriate or inappropriate. If we are mindful, we will recognize which it is, nurture appropriate attention, and release inappropriate attention, noting, "I am aware that this inappropriate attention will not benefit me or those I care about." When we know how to maintain a calm, joyful mind, our words and actions will manifest peace and happiness. We will be our own true friend and a good friend to many others.

Next, we use mindfulness to illuminate our speech. We may have resolved not to say certain things but then find ourselves saying them anyway. Mindfulness can help us stop before we say things that create conflict for ourselves and others.

Physical actions—a glance, a wave of the hand, the way we stand—also manifest our state of mind. Each gesture reveals our joy or sadness, love or hate, mindfulness or forgetfulness. Mindfulness illuminates what we are doing—how we stand and sit, how we look at others, how we smile, and how we frown. With the light of mindfulness present, we recognize which actions are beneficial and which are harmful. Actions that benefit us benefit others. Actions that harm us also harm others. That is why we begin this exercise by saying, "May I learn to look at myself with the eyes of understanding and compassion." Once you have used the key of understanding to open the door of love, you will experience acceptance for yourself and others. If you cannot accept others, it is because you do not yet accept yourself. If you are struggling with those around you, it is because there is a struggle inside of you. The *Lotus Sutra* advises us to look at all beings with the eyes of compassion. This includes ourselves.

"May I be able to recognize and touch the seeds of joy and happiness in myself" is an important practice. Our mind is described as the soil containing many seeds, positive and negative. We have to be aware of all of them. When we are in touch with our suffering, we have to know that there are other seeds, too. Our ancestors transmitted seeds of suffering to us, but also seeds of peace, freedom, joy, and happiness. Even if these seeds are buried deep in our consciousness, we can water them and help them grow stronger. Touching the seeds of joy, peace, freedom, solidity, and love within ourselves is an important practice, and we ask our friends to do the same for us. If we love someone, we have to recognize and touch the positive seeds in him every day, and refrain from watering the seeds of anger, despair, and hatred. That will help him grow in the direction of health and happiness.

When our practice has become solid and we are able to understand, love, and care for ourselves, at least to some extent, we can make others the object of our love meditation. First we take someone we like to be the object of our meditation; then, successively, someone neutral to us, someone we love, and someone we dislike very much. In the *Visuddhimagga,* Buddhaghosa advises us to start with someone we like, because it is easier to offer our mind of love to such a person. He uses the example of lighting a fire. First we ignite some straw. Once the straw is burning, we add small sticks. Once the small sticks have caught fire, we add small logs. Once those have caught fire, we add larger logs until even damp or green logs will burn. But if we try to start the fire with damp logs, we will not succeed. Buddhaghosa says that if we begin the practice with someone we are in love with, we may be overcome by strong feelings. He also advises us not to meditate on someone who has passed away. But if our mindfulness is solid and real, there is no need to worry. We can see that birth and death are just concepts, and we will not be carried away by meditating on someone we love, someone we despise, or someone who has passed away.

"May he/she be peaceful, happy, and light in body and in spirit. May he/she be free from injury. May he/she live in safety. May he/she be free from anger, disturbance, fear, worry, and anxiety." As you concentrate on another person as the object of your love meditation, if she lives east of you, send your energy to the east. If she is sitting to your right, extend your energy to the right. Surround her with the energy of love. Even if she is not in need of your love, practice this way. Dwell in deep concentration. Because you know how to love yourself, you have the capacity to offer love to someone you like. Look deeply into her five skandhas— body, feelings, perceptions, mental formations, and consciousness. This practice is quite easy.

In the *Satipatthana Sutta (Discourse on the Four Establishments of Mindfulness)*, the Buddha advises his monks to meditate on "the body in the body," "the feelings in the feelings," "the mind in the mind," and "the dharmas in the dharmas."[1] It means that when you meditate, you don't stand on the outside looking in. To have a deep and direct understanding of another person, you must become one with him or her. As long as you see yourself as separate from the object, your understanding is not yet true.

Once you succeed with the meditation on someone you like, select someone neutral to you to be the object of your meditation, someone you neither love nor hate, perhaps the mailman or the electrician. Even if you feel a little positively or negatively toward him, it is not exactly love or hatred. One neutral person can represent millions of others. Suppose you want to extend your love to the Bosnians. Take as the object of meditation one Bosnian man or woman you can visualize. Look deeply and visualize his body, feelings, perceptions, mental formations, and consciousness, and you will see the situation of his whole nation. If you can understand him, you can love and understand all the people of Bosnia. When you say, "May all beings be happy," if there is no clear or concrete subject, your wish may be too vague. It is easier to focus on one person and say, "May he and all those like him be safe and free from injury." Then your love will take hold in a real way.

---

[1] *Majjhima Nikaya*, Sutra 10. See Thich Nhat Hanh, *Transformation and Healing* (Berkeley: Parallax Press, 1990).

Love meditation is not wishful thinking. It is an authentic practice. Looking deeply, you radiate the energy of mindfulness onto the object of your meditation and illuminate it. True seeing always gives rise to true love.

A few months later, when you feel ready to move to the next stage of practice, take someone you love to be the object of your meditation. It can even be the person most dear to you. "May she be peaceful, happy, and light in body and spirit. May she be safe and free from injury. May she be free from anger, afflictions, fear, and anxiety." This practice is very sweet, and that is why the *Visuddhimagga* warns that it can have pitfalls. You can lose concentration while meditating on someone to whom you are too deeply attached.

Finally, meditate on someone you consider to be your enemy, someone whom just thinking about makes you angry. Put yourself in his place and give rise to the thought, "May he be peaceful, happy, and light in body and spirit." If you are not yet able to love yourself, you will not be able to love your enemy. But when you are able to love yourself, you can love anyone. When you do this, you will see that your so-called enemy is not more or less than a human being who is suffering. "May he be safe and free from injury." During the Vietnam War, I meditated on the Vietnamese soldiers, praying they would not be killed in battle. But I also meditated on the American soldiers and felt a very deep sympathy for them. I knew that they had been sent far away from home to kill or be killed, and I prayed for their safety. That led to a deep aspiration that the war would end and allow all Vietnamese and all Americans to live in peace. Once that aspiration was clear, there was only one path to take—to work for the end of the war. When you practice love meditation, you have to take that path. As soon as you see that the person you call your enemy is also suffering, you will be ready to love and accept him. The idea of "enemy" vanishes and is replaced by the reality of someone who is suffering and needs our love and compassion.

"May I be able to recognize and touch the seeds of joy and happiness in myself." First, learn to touch and identify the seeds of happiness and joy in yourself. When you are successful, even occasionally, continue with others. Even if the other person is extremely unhappy, you know that she has the seeds of joy and happiness in her. After you learn to water those seeds in yourself, you know how to do the same in her. Through your words, your glance, the touch of your hand, your loving care, you will be able to help her touch those seeds, and that will help her, and it will help you also.

At Plum Village, the students were asked to write down all the positive attributes of their parents. One young man had no difficulty with his father, but he was hesitant to write about his mother, because he thought that it would be too unpleasant. He was surprised when he began the meditation and was able to touch many positive qualities in his mother. The more positive things he discovered, the more his resentment subsided. Penetrating this meditation, he reestablished his connection with his mother, and love flowed from his heart.

After that, he wrote his mother a love letter based on his insights. He acknowledged the positive qualities in her and expressed gratitude for her presence. When his mother received this letter, she was deeply moved. Her son had never talked to her so positively before. She told a neighbor about it and about how happy she was to have her son again, and she expressed regret that her mother was not still alive. She wanted to write a similar letter to her own mother. When the young man learned of this, he wrote, "Do not think Grandma has passed away. She is still alive in you. Please write to her. I am sure she will read your letter, even as you are writing it." He got this insight from the practice—our parents and all our ancestors are alive in us. We are a construction of them. After receiving his second letter, his mother did write to her mother. One person practicing can help the whole family.

"May I be able to recognize and touch the seeds of joy and happiness in myself." *Sarvabijaka* ("all the seeds") is a word used in Buddhism to describe our consciousness. We are the gardeners who identify, water, and cultivate the best seeds. We need some faith that there are good seeds within us, and then, with appropriate attention, we need to touch those seeds while we practice sitting meditation, walking meditation, and throughout the day. When we succeed in touching our positive seeds once, we will know how to touch them again and again, and they will strengthen. That is the reason I often ask psychotherapists not just to discuss problems with their clients, but to help clients also touch their own seeds of joy and happiness. If a therapist knows how to walk mindfully and touch the wholesome elements in herself, she will know how to help her clients do the same. Why not take your clients outside for walking meditation? Show them how to make refreshing steps on the earth and touch the blue sky and the white clouds. Show them how to nourish themselves by slowing down and enjoying the simple pleasures that are available right in the present moment. It can be too destructive if therapists and clients only talk about suffering.

"May I be able to recognize and touch the seeds of joy and happiness in myself." The nature of this exercise is love. "Many people today do not know how to practice true love." This is a sentence in the book of training for novice monks and nuns.[2]

"May I learn to identify and see the sources of anger, craving, and delusion in myself." "To identify" means to recognize the presence of something. "To see the sources" means to understand its nature—where it came from, what circumstances made it arise, and how long it has been there. This is a process of deep looking.

There are poisons inside us, including craving, anger, and delusion. Craving is the greed that makes us chase after fame, advantage, wealth, and sex. Delusion is ignorance, the lack of understanding. In addition to these three poisons, there are others, including arrogance and suspicion. We have to practice mindfulness in our everyday lives to know craving, anger, and delusion are present in ourselves and to see how much suffering is caused by these poisons (and not just by outside circumstances). The Buddha asked, "How can anger arise in one who has no anger?" The primary cause of anger is the seed of anger in ourselves. Two people might hear the same words and see the same things, yet only one becomes angry. Words and events only stimulate what is inside us. If there were no seeds of anger in our store consciousness, anger could not arise.

We need to master our own anger before we can help others do the same. When the flames of anger flare up, we tend to lash out at those who have watered our seeds of anger. It is like finding our house on fire and, instead of putting out the flames, chasing those we think started it.

---

[2] Thich Nhat Hanh, *Stepping into Freedom: An Introduction to Buddhist Monastic Training* (Berkeley: Parallax Press, 1997).

Arguing with others only waters the seeds of anger in us. When anger rises, return to yourself and use the energy of mindfulness to embrace, soothe, and illuminate it. Do not think you will feel better if you can make the other person suffer, too. This is a dangerous way of thinking. In their anger, the other person might respond even more harshly, and the anger will escalate. The Buddha taught that when anger arises, close your eyes and ears, return to yourself, and tend to the source of anger within. Transforming your anger is not just for your personal liberation. Everyone around you and even those more distant will benefit if you succeed.

The Buddha listed seven reasons for us to let our anger go:

1. Anger makes us ugly. If, when we get angry, we look in the mirror, we will do something to look more beautiful. This short verse can help us practice:

*Knowing that anger makes me ugly,*
*I smile instead.*
*I return to myself*
*and meditate on love.[3]*

2. Anger makes us suffer. We double up in pain "like a shrimp being roasted."

3. We are unable to develop or flourish.

4. We fail to prosper materially or spiritually. We lose whatever riches or happiness we had.

5. We become known only for our anger.

---

[3] See Thich Nhat Hanh, *Present Moment Wonderful Moment* (Berkeley: Parallax Press, 1990), p. 66.

6. We lose our friends, because they fear being blown apart by the bomb inside us.

7. We become a hungry ghost, unable to take part in a fresh, joyful Sangha.[4]

When you are angry, your face looks like a bomb about to go off. Close your eyes and ears and return to yourself in order to quell the flames. Smile, even if it takes effort. Smiling relaxes hundreds of tiny muscles, making your face more attractive. Sit wherever you are, and look deeply. If your concentration is not yet strong, you can go outside and practice walking meditation. Most essential is to water the seed of mindfulness and allow it to arise in your mind consciousness.

Mindfulness is always mindfulness of something, just as anger is always anger at something. When you drink a glass of water and are aware that you are drinking a glass of water, that is mindfulness of drinking water. In this case, we produce mindfulness of anger. "Breathing in, I know I am angry. Breathing out, I know that anger is in me." First the energy of anger arises, and second the energy of mindfulness arises. The second energy embraces the first in order to soothe it and allow it to subside. We do not produce mindfulness to chase away or fight our anger but to take good care of it. This method is non-dualistic and nonviolent. It is non-dualistic because it recognizes that mindfulness and anger are both parts of ourselves. One energy embraces the other. Don't be angry at your anger. Don't try to chase it away or suppress it. Acknowledge that it has

[4] *Kodhana Sutta, Anguttara Nikaya, Sattaka Nipata* ("Chapter on Seven Things"), Sutta 60 (Vol. IV, p. 94).

arisen and take care of it. When your stomach hurts, you don't get angry at it. You take care of it. When a mother hears her baby crying, she puts down what she is doing, picks the baby up, and comforts her. Then she tries to understand why the baby is crying, whether it is because of some physical or emotional discomfort.

Look deeply at your anger as you would at your own child. Do not reject it or hate it. Meditation is not to turn yourself into a battlefield, one side opposing the other. Conscious breathing soothes and calms the anger, and mindfulness penetrates it. Within fifteen minutes of lighting the heater, the warm air pervades the cold room, and a transformation occurs. You don't need to discard or repress anything, not even your anger. Anger is just an energy, and all energies can be transformed. Meditation is the art of using one kind of energy to transform another. The instant the mother holds her child, the child feels the energy of love and comfort and begins to feel relief. Even if the cause of discomfort is still present, being held in mindfulness is enough to provide some relief.

In the *Anapanasati Sutta (Discourse on the Full Awareness of Breathing)*, the Buddha teaches, "Breathing in, I calm the activities of the mind in me." "Activities of the mind" refers to any emotional or psychological state, such as anger, sadness, jealousy, or fear. As you breathe in and out mindfully, you embrace and calm that mental state. As soon as you are aware that anger has arisen, produce mindfulness to embrace the anger. After ten minutes, the intensity of the anger will lessen, and mindfulness will reveal many things. After holding her baby for a few minutes, perhaps humming a lullaby, the mother will search for the cause of the discomfort. Perhaps the baby has a fever or a chill, perhaps her diaper is too tight, or she is thirsty. As soon as the mother discovers the cause, she can transform the situation right away. It is important to get at the root of the problem. This is the practice of looking deeply.

"Breathing in, I know I am angry. Breathing out, I know that the anger is in me." First, you practice recognition. "Hello, anger, my old friend." Then you look deeply to see its source. "Why am I angry?" The first thing you will discover is that your suffering has its roots in your store consciousness, in seeds that are already there, seeds of anger, delusion, pride, suspicion, or greed. The other person is only a secondary cause. The next thing you will see is that the other person is also suffering. You may have thought you were the only one suffering, but that is not correct. When someone spills that kind of suffering onto you, you know that he is suffering. When you understand this, love will well up in you, and you will want to help. Understanding is the key.

Thanks to the practice of mindfulness, your anger will return to your store consciousness. The next time it arises, practice the same way, and eventually that seed of anger in you will weaken. This is the practice of facing your anger, and, thanks to mindfulness, transforming it into the energies of love and understanding.

One day when the Buddha was staying in the Jeta Grove, near Shravasti, Shariputra invited the other monks to gather together, and he told them, "Brothers, there are five kinds of situations in which anger could arise, but can be avoided.

"The first is when someone's actions, but not his words, irritate us. There are people we cannot stand the sight of. The way they stand and the way they move irritate us, but when they speak, their words are not at all offensive. When you are with someone like that, listen to his words but ignore his actions. If you dwell on his actions, anger will arise, but if you pay attention only to his words, your anger will subside. There was a monk who liked to sew his robes from scraps of cloth he found in garbage heaps. Every time he saw a tiny scrap, even if the heap was rife with the stench of urine or feces, he would pick it up, carry it back to the monastery, wash it, and sew it to other scraps to make a robe. It was difficult to watch him do this, but, at the same time, his speech was friendly. If you dwell on his speech, anger will not arise in you.

"The second situation is that of someone who speaks with as much venom as a snake, but whose actions are friendly and helpful. Pay attention to such a person's actions and ignore his words. Near here is a deep lake covered with straw, grass, leaves, duckweed, and twigs. Someone overcome by heat might go to that lake for a swim. After disrobing on the shore, he pushes aside the straw, grass, leaves, duckweed, and twigs and steps into the clear, cool water. It would be a pity to refuse the coolness of the lake just because of a little straw, grass, leaves, duckweed, and twigs.

"The third situation is that of a person whose actions and words are both unpleasant. Look very carefully at such a person and try to find some positive qualities, even if they are not immediately apparent. Everyone has some positive qualities. This practice is more difficult, but not impossible. Imagine a man who has traveled hundreds of miles on foot, whose throat is parched with thirst. He comes across an imprint in the ground formed by a water buffalo's foot, with a tiny bit of water in it. He says to himself, 'If I try to scoop that water using a leaf, it may spill. So I'll bend over and suck it directly from the puddle.' After that, the man feels refreshed enough to continue his journey. We have to look deeply to find some positive qualities in those whose speech and actions are both unpleasant. If we can find any, we will be able to accept them. Though this situation is more difficult than the first or second, the wise will be able to let go of their dislike for such persons.

"The fourth situation is that of someone whose actions, words, and thoughts are all unwholesome. On a remote country road, there is a traveler who falls deathly ill. There is no nearby village, and he is utterly alone, with no one to look after him. There is no hope he will survive. But suddenly, another traveler passes by. He sees the desperate man lying alongside the road, and he stops, his heart filled with compassion. He helps the man up and supports him, step by step, until they reach the next village. Then the traveler finds a doctor and stays with the man for three or four weeks until the illness is cured. The traveler rejoices in the man's recovery. When we encounter someone whose actions, speech, and thoughts are all disagreeable, we can be certain that person is filled with suffering. If we don't love him, if we don't help him, who will? If love is in our heart, we will be able to accept those whose actions, speech, and thoughts are all disagreeable.

"The fifth situation is that of a person whose actions, speech, and thoughts are all wholesome. Beside a village is a lake filled with fragrant pink and white lotus flowers. The shore is covered with soft green grass, and surrounding the lake is a park filled with shade trees in which birds sing and butterflies flutter. It is truly a paradise. If you live near such a lake but do not come and sit along its shore, don't swim in it, don't scoop up its clear water in your hands to drink, you do not know how to live happily. When you encounter someone whose actions, speech, and thoughts are all wholesome and kind, resolve to spend time by his side."[5]

It is important to look deeply into the suffering of others. Someone whose actions are unkind, whose thoughts are unwholesome, whose speech is unwholesome is certainly suffering a lot. When you look deeply and see this suffering, your heart will open and the key of understanding will reveal itself. So many people in our society were molested as children, and they continue to suffer their whole lives. Their fear and hatred never cease, and their self-esteem remains very low. If such people can learn to look deeply at their abuser's pain, if they can see the source of these unwholesome acts, see that their abusers are prisoners of a mind poisoned by anger, craving, and delusion, their hearts may open and their fear and hatred will gradually subside.

Four years ago, a young man came to Plum Village who was extremely angry at his father. At that time, the residents were practicing love meditation and writing letters to those with whom they had difficulties. There is an exercise in *The Blooming of a Lotus* about meditating on a five-year-old child: "Seeing myself as a five-year-old child, I breathe in. Smiling to the five-year-old child, I breathe out."[6] That five year old is still inside you, and he may have suffered a lot, but when you get in touch with him, your heart will fill with compassion.

---

[5] *The Sutra on the Water Simile, Madhagama* 25, *Taisho* 26. Also, *Aghata Vinaya Sutta, Anguttara Nikaya,* III, 186. Also, *Dutiya-Aghatapativinaya Sutta, Anguttara Nikaya, Pañcaka Nipata* ("Chapter on Five Things"), (Vol. III, p. 186).

[6] Boston: Beacon Press, 1993, p. 79.

A five year old is very fragile and easily wounded. So many parents raise their children without mindfulness. They dump all their pain and anger on them, and by the age of five, the child is already filled with fear and sorrow. She may try to express those feelings to her parents, but her parents do not have the capacity to hear. A child so young does not have the capacity to explain her suffering. As she stumbles over her words, her mother might interrupt her or even shout. Such language is like ice water thrown over a tender heart. The child may never try to confide in her parents again, and the wound remains deep. Parents repeat acts like this over and over until their connection with their children is severed. The cause is the lack of mindfulness. If a father doesn't know how to control his anger, he may cut off communication with his son, and the son may suffer for his whole life, and himself be unable to communicate with teachers, friends, and, later, his own son.

I asked the young man to meditate on himself as a five year old for one week, and then I gave him this exercise: "Breathing in, I see my father as a five-year-old child. Breathing out, I smile at the five-year-old child my father was." We all have an image of our father as an adult, but we forget that he was once a little boy whose feelings were also easily hurt. Please practice this meditation. If it helps, find a photo of your father as a five year old and look at it. Breathe in and out and smile at your father as a five year old. You will see that your father carries wounds in himself just like yours. In that moment, you *become* your father.

When he spoke about the Four Immeasurable Minds, the Buddha used the term *sabbattataya*—"being one with everything."[7] You become one with the object of your contemplation, in this case you become your father. If you look deeply, you will understand that when he was a five-year-old child, your father was deeply hurt by the cruel behavior of others. If he was hurt as a child and never learned how to transform those wounds, it is only natural that he will inflict his pain on others, including you. His own child becomes a victim of his suffering, just as he was the victim of his parents' suffering.

The young man placed a photo of his father on the desk in his room at Plum Village, and every time he entered the room, he would look into his father's eyes and practice getting to know the man who had been such a stranger to him. He smiled, feeling sympathy towards his father as a child in pain. Before leaving the room, he would look at his father's picture again and breathe mindfully.

One day, he wrote a letter to his father, even though his father had already passed away. As he was writing it, his heart suddenly opened, and he felt a great burden lift. He had seen into his father's suffering, and he forgave him. Love and compassion became authentic energies in him and longing to reconcile with his father was no longer just a wish. The poison of anger had dissolved. This is very much like Shariputra's meditation. By looking deeply at the suffering of another person and understanding the sources of his pain, the door of love and understanding was opened.

To practice this exercise, begin by learning to touch the positive seeds that lie within you, and also the seeds of suffering. Recognize that they are there, and look deeply to

---

[7] *Majjhima Nikaya,* Sutra 99.

understand their nature—their root causes. Once you understand the roots of your suffering—your anger, your hurt, your frustration—your heart becomes peaceful, calm, and light. The roots of anger in you are transformed, and it becomes easy to accept and love. You have succeeded in extinguishing the fires in yourself, and you can help others do the same. Touching the seeds of joy and happiness in ourselves, identifying and seeing the sources of anger, craving, and delusion in ourselves, we truly become peaceful, happy, and light in body and spirit; safe and free from injury; and free from anger, afflictions, fear, and anxiety.

# CHAPTER FIVE

# *Nourishing Happiness*

THESE THREE EXERCISES ARE ALSO ALONG THE LINES OF THE *Visuddhimagga:*

> *May I know how to nourish the seeds of joy in myself every day.*
> *May he/she know how to nourish the seeds of joy in him/ herself every day.*
> *May they know how to nourish the seeds of joy in themselves every day.*

> *May I be able to live fresh, solid, and free.*
> *May he/she be able to live fresh, solid, and free.*
> *May they be able to live fresh, solid, and free.*

> *May I be free from attachment and aversion, but not be indifferent.*
> *May he/she be free from attachment and aversion, but not be indifferent.*
> *May they be free from attachment and aversion, but not be indifferent.*

These meditations help us water the seeds of joy and happiness in our store consciousness. Joy and happiness are the food of a Zen monk. Before eating, we say, "May all beings be nourished by the joy of meditation."

What is the nature of this joy? How can we touch true joy in every moment of our lives? How can we live in a way that brings a smile, the eyes of love, and happiness to everyone we encounter? Use your talent to find ways to bring happiness to yourself and others—the happiness that arises from meditation and not from the pursuit of fruitless pleasure-seeking. Meditative joy has the capacity to nourish our mindfulness, understanding, and love. Try to live in a way that encourages deep happiness in yourself and others. "I vow to bring joy to one person in the morning and to help relieve the suffering of one person in the afternoon." Ask yourself, "Who can I make smile this morning?" This is the art of creating happiness.

The *Samiddhi Sutra* is the story of a young monk. Early one morning, Samiddhi went to the river to bathe, and as he was drying himself, a goddess *(devi)* appeared and asked him, "Bhikkhu, you are so young. Why did you become a renunciate in the prime of your life? Why don't you go out and enjoy your youth?" Samiddhi replied, "Dear devi, I am very happy. I practice the Buddha's teaching to live happily in the present moment. Chasing after the five worldly pleasures—running after fame, wealth, sex, sleep, or food—do not bring lasting happiness. I practice mindfulness in my daily life, and I experience deep peace, freedom, and joy." Four important subjects are discussed in the *Samiddhi Sutra:* the *idea* of happiness, the existence of real joy, the practice of reliance, and the trap of complexes.[1]

---

[1] *Samiddhi Sutra, Samyuktagama,* 1078, *Taisho* 99. Also, *Samiddhi Sutta, Samyutta Nikaya,* Vol. I, p. 8.

Our notions about happiness entrap us. We forget that they are just ideas. Our idea of happiness can prevent us from actually being happy. We fail to see the opportunity for joy that is right in front of us when we are caught in a belief that happiness should take a particular form.

The second subject discussed in the sutra is the existence of real joy. The goddess asked the young monk Samiddhi why he chose to abandon happiness in the present moment for a vague promise of happiness in the future, and Samiddhi answered, "The opposite is true. It is the idea of happiness in the future that I have abandoned, so I can dwell deeply in the present moment." Samiddhi explained how unwholesome desires ultimately bring about anxiety and sorrow, while a life of wholesome joys bring happiness right in the present moment. The sutra uses the term *akalika,* "freedom from time."

The third important subject in the *Samiddhi Sutra* is the practice of reliance, or support. Relying on the Dharma is not just an idea. When you live in accord with the Dharma, the Buddha's way of understanding and love, you realize joy, tranquility, stability, and freedom. Relying on the Dharma can also be called "taking refuge in the island of self," the island of peace in each of us. We have to learn how to return to that island when we need to. When the Buddha was about to pass away, he told the assembly of monks and nuns, "My dear friends, take refuge in the island of self. Do not take refuge in anything else. When you go back to that island, you will find Buddha, Dharma, and Sangha there."

*Being an island unto myself.*
*As an island unto myself.*

*Buddha is my mindfulness.*
*Shining near, shining far.*
*Dharma is my breathing,*
*guarding body and mind.*
*I am free.*

*Being an island unto myself.*
*As an island unto myself.*
*Sangha is my skandhas,*
*working in harmony.*
*Taking refuge in myself.*
*Coming back to myself.*
*I am free.*

Although this practice can be used anywhere, at any time, it is especially useful when we are in a state of anxiety and don't know what to do. When we practice, we are transported to the calmest, most stable place we can go. The island of self is mindfulness, our awakened nature, the foundation of stability and calm that resides in us and shines light on our path. When our five skandhas are in harmony, we will naturally act in ways that bring peace. Conscious breathing brings about this evenness. Can anything else be more important?

The fourth important subject in the sutra concerns the trap of complexes—thinking you are better, worse than, or equal to others. All of these complexes arise because we think we are a separate self. Happiness built on the notion of a separate self is weak and unreliable. Through the practice of meditation, we come to see that we "inter-are" with all other beings, and our fears, anxieties, anger, and sorrow disappear. If you practice true happiness, relying on the

Dharma and realizing the interconnected and interdependent nature of all things, you become freer and more stable every day. Gradually you will be in a paradise where the deep love described by the Buddha pervades. The Buddha's teachings on love are authentic and complete. This kind of love always leads to true happiness.

Happiness is not an individual matter; it has the nature of interbeing. When you are able to make one friend smile, her happiness will nourish you also. When you find ways to peace, joy, and happiness, you do it for everyone. Begin by nourishing yourself with joyful feelings. Practice walking meditation outside, enjoying the fresh air, the trees, the stars in the night sky. What do you do to nourish yourself? It is important to discuss this subject with dear friends to find concrete ways to nourish joy and happiness.

When you succeed in doing this, your suffering, sorrow, and painful mental formations will begin to transform. When your body is invaded by harmful bacteria, your own antibodies surround the bacteria and render them harmless. When there aren't enough antibodies, your body will create more so it can neutralize the infection. Likewise, when you suffuse your body and mind with feelings of the joy of meditation, your body and spirit will be strengthened. Joyous feelings have a capacity to transform the feelings of sorrow and pain in us.

Please also practice, "May I know how to nourish the seeds of joy in him or her every day." Insert the name of the person you've chosen—your friend, brother, sister, or teacher—and nourish the seeds of joy in him or her. We often need to unburden ourselves of our suffering by sharing it with someone we trust. But we mustn't forget that she may be coping with her own pain and needs to be nourished by feelings of joy herself. If we pour our suffering onto her, she may become exhausted. If we want to rely on her for future support, we need to be careful not to pile too much suffering on her. She will reach her limit and will not be able to take it anymore.

Learn to nourish yourself and the other person with joy. Are you able to make her smile? Are you able to increase her faith and enthusiasm? If you are not able to do these small things for her, how can you say you love her? To love someone means to bring her joy and happiness in concrete ways. If you act skillfully, your words and actions will make her feel fresh and light. Sometimes a kind word or two are enough to help her blossom like a flower.

Practice first with someone you like, then with someone you love, and someone you feel neutral about. Once you have looked deeply into that person and understood his deepest needs, he will no longer be a neutral person. Finally, make a person you hate the object of your meditation. At first you despise him, but after you have used mindfulness to look deeply into that person, understanding and insight will bring about love and compassion. The person you once hated will become someone you feel love towards.

Practicing this meditation, our love will soon surround and permeate all five categories of people, and the distinctions between those you hate and those dear to you will disappear. Your meditation will succeed even with those you have hated in the past. The five categories become equal. The bodhisattva regards the dear and not dear equally, and does not bear a heart of hatred even towards those who have behaved thoughtlessly and cruelly. If you don't practice the Four Immeasurable Minds, how will you ever be able to regard someone dear and someone not dear equally?

"May I know how to nourish the seeds of joy in myself every day. May he/she know how to nourish the seeds of joy in him/herself every day. May I know how to nourish the seeds of joy in the person I hate and help the person I hate nourish the seeds of joy in him or herself." When you give rise to such a mind, anger and hatred will vanish from within you, and you will have true peace and joy. As long as traces of hatred and anger are in you, you will not be able to find true peace. When you are finally able to love your enemy, you may feel like a great hero, but then you will see that, in truth, to love that person is to love your own self. When you open your heart and accept the person you once hated, quite naturally your heart will experience ease and you will be the first to receive the benefits. This is the true meaning of equanimity—equality without discrimination or prejudice.

"May I be able to live fresh, solid, and free." "Fresh" is a translation of the Vietnamese word for "cool, without fever." We know how uncomfortable we feel when we are feverish. Jealousy, anger, and harmful desires are a kind of fever. The Universal Door chapter of the *Lotus Sutra* states that whenever a fire burns, if you recite the name of Avalokiteshvara, that fire is transformed into a lotus pond. If someone hurls you into a fire pit with their words or actions, recite the name of Avalokiteshvara and the fire pit will become a cool lotus pond. Avalokiteshvara represents the energy of love and compassion. If you are trapped in the flames of anger, hatred, harmful passion, jealousy, and suspicion, meditate on the Four Immeasurable Minds and those flames will stop burning. You will find yourself swimming in a cool, clear lake.

When we are caught in the trap of the Five Harmful Desires,[2] we will be burned. We have to know our limits. As a protection, we practice the Five Mindfulness Trainings and take refuge in a Sangha. Every autumn, thousands of migrating wood pigeons fly over Plum Village in formation. Any wood pigeon that breaks away and flies separately can easily fall into danger. There are hunters near Plum Village who lure the birds down using pigeons. The wood pigeons leave their formation and become easy targets for the hunters. The same is true for us. If we think we can live alone without the support of a Sangha, we are not aware of our limits. Practicing with a Sangha is like bathing in a refreshing stream, provided we know how to organize the Sangha well and how to live together harmoniously. It is easy to cultivate seeds of joy in our life of practice. This requires the intelligence, insight, and the organizational talents of every member of the Sangha. When any Sangha member has an idea that can bring joy and happiness to the community, he or she should share this with everyone.

"May I be able to live fresh, solid, and free." Solid here refers to stability, which is one of the characteristics of Nirvana. If you are not solid, you will not be able to accomplish much. Each day you only need to take a few solid steps in the direction of your goal. If you are a monk or a nun, you remember your vow to devote your life to practicing the Dharma in order to bring joy and happiness to all beings. To realize your vow, you must study, practice, live within a Sangha, and take stable steps each day along that path.

---

[2] Money, sex, fame, overeating, oversleeping.

Every morning, you rededicate yourself to your path in order not to go astray. Before going to sleep at night, you take a few minutes to review the day. "Did I live in the direction of my ideals today?" If you see that you took two or three steps in that direction, that is good enough. If you did not, say to yourself, "I'll do better tomorrow." The next morning when you wake up, resolve to take solid steps in the direction of your ideals. Don't compare yourself with others. Just look to yourself to see whether you are going in the direction you cherish.

If you want your life to be more solid each day, take refuge in things that are solid. If you lean on something that is not solid, you will fall. The Three Jewels—Buddha, Dharma and Sangha—are very solid; if you take refuge in the Three Jewels, you will be solid also. Build your house on a strong foundation, not on mud or sand. A few Sanghas may not yet be solid, but usually taking refuge in a Sangha is a wise thing to do. Sangha members everywhere are practicing earnestly. Our faith will be strengthened when we recognize the strength of the Sangha that extends throughout space and time.

"May I be able to live fresh, solid and free." Freedom here means to transcend the trap of harmful desires. Monks and nuns enjoy and benefit from that kind of freedom. Freedom here means to be without attachments—whether to a temple, a diploma, or a certain rank. From time we time, we encounter people who are very free. They can do whatever is needed, unattached to anything.

"May I be free from attachment and aversion, but not be indifferent." When we are indifferent, nothing is enjoyable, interesting, or worth striving for. We do not experience love or understanding, and our life has no joy or meaning. We do not even notice the beauty of the autumn leaves or the laughter of children nearby. We are unable to touch the suffering or the happiness of others. If you find yourself in a state of indifference, ask your friends for help. Even with all its suffering, life is filled with many wonders. Birth and death are miracles, and beneath the waves of birth and death lies the wondrous ultimate dimension.

Just before my disciple Chân Sinh (True Life) died in Montréal, I sent him this verse:

*Suchness is the ultimate reality.*
*How can birth and death touch you?*
*Awaken early to the pink dawn.*
*Peace comes without effort.*

Beneath the poem, I wrote, "Brother Chân Sinh, I am holding your hand so that together, teacher and student, we can transcend every pain and danger."

Birth is wondrous, so is death, and so is the ultimate reality that underlies both. If you can touch that wonder, you will no longer be indifferent, and little by little, you will become solid and free in your attitude and your life.

"May I be free from attachment and aversion." The kind of love the Buddha wanted us to cultivate was not possessive or attached. All of us, young and old, have a tendency to become attached. As soon as we are born, ignorance and attachment to self are already there. Whenever we love someone, we tend to become possessive. When we are loved, we want to be the sole object of our lover's attention. We don't want her to love anyone else. Possessive love is like a dictatorship. We want to control the one we love, dictating what they can and cannot do. In wholesome love relationships, there is a certain amount of possessiveness and attachment, but if it is excessive, both lover and beloved will suffer.

A father may think he "owns" his son. "You have to obey everything I say. Study this, do that, or I will not recognize you as my son." A young man may say to his girlfriend, "You can't go shopping at that hour, you can't use that perfume, you can't wear that color." When you love in such a toxic way, it is like putting chains on your lover. The love that once seemed a castle becomes nothing more than a prison. When the paint begins to peel, the prison bars are revealed, and both feel trapped, unable to escape. Your marriage contract may have become a life sentence with no possibility of release. Separating or staying together, both are intolerable. This is true not only of marriages, but also in relationships between parents and children, friends, teachers, and students. It is essential that we learn to love in a way that preserves our beloved's freedom and allows us both to maintain our individuality. That is the kind of love the Buddha taught.

What should you do if you are already in a love relationship ruled by possessiveness, dictatorship, and attachment? Practice deep looking to identify the extent to which your love is despotic and attached. Have you ever run over a rope with a lawn mower? It can take an hour or more to untangle the rope, to free the blades to turn again. Attachment is like that. It obstructs the flow of life. Look deeply to discover the nature of your love. When you have identified the degree of attachment, despotism, and possessiveness in your love, you can begin untangling the knots. Removing a little of the dictatorship, the attachment, and the possessiveness will relieve some of the suffering. Though you may not be happy yet, lessening the suffering is a good start. You suffered ninety-nine percent of the time before, and now it is only eighty percent. That is already significant. We suffer from indifference and the lack of love, but we suffer far more from attachment.

Without mindfulness, attachment will surely become aversion. When love is still new, we think that life without our beloved would be intolerable. But when attachment becomes aversion, life with our beloved is intolerable, and divorce seems to be the only option. The poles of attachment and aversion both lead to suffering. Even if you divorce your spouse or disown your child, the sources of suffering remain intact. When you enter a new relationship or have another child, the attached and controlling way you love will infect the new situation and bring about the same kinds of suffering. The problem is not whether to get divorced or disown your child. The problem is to look deeply at the nature of your loving to identify the negative elements of attachment and possessiveness in it and to see how your way of looking, loving, speaking, and acting have to change so that true love, compassion, joy, and equanimity can enter. When you practice in this way, your positive qualities will slowly increase.

If we practice according to the teachings of the Buddha and with the support of a Sangha, we will learn the nature of love, compassion, joy, and equanimity. The seeds of these qualities are already in our store consciousness. Studying and practicing the Four Immeasurable Minds will water those seeds in us. Through the practice of deep looking, the seeds of suffering, pain, sadness, and attachment will shrink to make room for the expanding positive seeds.

Do not say, "Love, compassion, joy, and equanimity are the way saints love. Since I'm not a saint, I cannot possibly love that way." The Buddha and the bodhisattvas practiced in the same way we do. At first, their love was tainted with attachment, desire to control, and possessiveness. But thanks to the practice they were able to transform those poisons and arrive at a love that is spacious, all-encompassing, and marvelous.

The Buddha's teachings on love are clear. It is possible to live twenty-four hours a day in a state of love. Every movement, every glance, every thought, and every word can be infused with love. The Four Immeasurable Minds are strong concentrations *(samadhi):* the concentration of love, the concentration of compassion, the concentration of joy, and the concentration of equanimity. When you dwell in these concentrations, you are living in the most beautiful, peaceful, and joyous realm in the universe. If someone asks your address, you can say "the abodes of Brahma"—the Immeasurable Minds of love, compassion, joy, and equanimity. There are five-star hotels that cost more than $2,000 per night, yet the abode of Brahma offers more happiness than these. It is a five-thousand-star hotel, a place where we can learn to love and be loved.

CHAPTER SIX

# *True Love*

TRUE LOVE CONTAINS RESPECT. IN THE VIETNAMESE TRADITION, husband and wife always respect each other as honored guests. When you practice this, your love will last for a long time. In Vietnamese, the words *tinh* and *nghiã* both mean love. Tinh contains a lot of passion. Nghiã is calmer, more understanding, more faithful. You are not as passionate, but your love is deeper and more solid. You are more willing to sacrifice to make the other person happy. Nghiã is the result of sharing difficulties and joys over a long period of time.

You begin with passion, but, living with each other, you learn to deal with difficulties, and your love deepens. The passion diminishes, but nghiã increases all the time. You understand the other person better, and you feel a lot of gratitude: "Thank you for being my husband (my wife), for having chosen me as your companion to share your best qualities, as well as your suffering. While I was having difficulty and remained awake deep into the night, you took care of me. You showed me that my well-being is your own well-being. You did the impossible to help me get well. I am deeply grateful." When a couple stays together for a long time, it is because of nghiã. Nghiã is the kind of love we really need for our family and for our society. With nghiã, you are sure the other person will love you and take care of you "until your hair becomes white and your teeth fall out." Nghiã is built by both of you in your daily life.

Look deeply to see which of these elements are in your love. You cannot say love is one hundred percent tinh or one hundred percent nghiã. Both are in it. Look into the eyes of your beloved and ask deeply, "Who are you, my love, who has come to me and taken my suffering as your suffering, my happiness as your happiness, my life and death as your life and death? Who are you whose self has become my self? Why aren't you a dewdrop, a butterfly, a bird, a pine tree?" Ask with your whole body and mind. Later, you will have to ask the person who causes you the most suffering the same questions: "Who are you who brings me such pain, who makes me feel so much anger and hatred?" To understand, you have to become one with your beloved, and also one with your so-called enemy. You have to worry about what they worry about, suffer their suffering, appreciate what they appreciate. You and the object of your love cannot be two. They are as much you as you are yourself.

Continue until you see yourself in the cruelest person on Earth, in the child starving, in the political prisoner. Practice until you recognize yourself in everyone in the supermarket, on the street corner, in a concentration camp, on a leaf, in a dewdrop. Meditate until you see yourself in a speck of dust in a distant galaxy. See and listen with the whole of your being. If you are fully present, the rain of the Dharma will water the deepest seeds in your store consciousness, and tomorrow, while you are washing the dishes or looking at the blue sky, that seed will spring forth, and love and understanding will appear as a beautiful flower.

*Being rock, being gas, being mist, being mind,*
*being the mesons traveling among the galaxies*
*at the speed of light,*
*you have come here, my beloved.*
*And your blue eyes shine, so beautiful, so deep.*
*You have taken the path traced for you*
*from the non-beginning and the never-ending.*
*You say that on your way here*
*you have gone through*
*many millions of births and deaths.*
*Innumerable times you have been transformed*
*into firestorms in outer space.*
*You have used your own body*
*to measure the age of the mountains and rivers.*
*You have manifested yourself*
*as trees, grass, butterflies, single-celled beings,*
*and as chrysanthemums.*
*But the eyes with which you look at me this morning*
*tell me that you have never died.*
*Your smile invites me into the game*
*whose beginning no one knows,*
*the game of hide-and-seek.*


*O green caterpillar, you are solemnly using your body*
*to measure the length of the rose branch that grew up last*
    *Summer.*
*Everyone says that you, my beloved, were just born this*
    *Spring.*
*Tell me, how long have you been around?*
*Why wait until this moment to reveal yourself to me,*
*carrying with you that smile which is so silent and so deep?*
*O caterpillar, suns, moons, and stars flow out*

*each time I exhale.*
*Who knows that the infinitely large must be found*
*in your tiny body?*
*Upon each point on your body,*
*thousands of Buddha fields have been established.*
*With each stretch of your body, you measure time*
*from the non-beginning to the never-ending.*
*The great mendicant of old is still there on Vulture Peak,*
*contemplating the ever-splendid sunset.*

*Gautama, how strange!*
*Who said that the Udumbara flower blooms*
*only once every 3,000 years?*

*The sound of the rising tide—you cannot help hearing it*
*if you have an attentive ear.[1]*

If you really love someone, you have to be fully present for him or her. A ten-year-old boy I know was asked by his father what he wanted for his birthday, and he said, "Daddy, I want you!" His father was too busy. He had no time for his family. His son knew that the greatest gift his father could offer was his true presence.

When you are concentrated—mind and body at one—anything you say can be a mantra. It does not have to be spoken in Sanskrit. It can be uttered in your own language: "Darling, I am here for you." If you are fully present, this mantra will produce a miracle. You become real, the per-

---

[1] I wrote this poem many years ago. Joanna Macy called it a love poem. The "old mendicant" is Shakyamuni Buddha. See *Call Me by My True Names: The Collected Poems of Thich Nhat Hanh* (Berkeley: Parallax Press, 1993), pp. 130–131.

son you say it to becomes real, and life becomes real in that moment. You bring happiness to yourself and to the other person. This is the greatest gift you can offer your loved one. To love is to be there for him, for her, and for them.

"I know you are there, and I am very happy" is a second mantra. When I look deeply at the moon, I breathe in and out deeply and say, "Full moon, I know you are there, and I am very happy." I do the same when I see the morning star. Walking among the beautiful spring magnolia trees in Korea, I looked at the beautiful flowers and said, "I know you are there, and I am very happy." To be truly present and know that the other is also there is a miracle. Whenever you are really there, you are able to recognize and appreciate the presence of the other—the full moon, the morning star, the magnolia flowers, the person you love the most. First practice breathing in and out mindfully to recover yourself. Then sit close to the one you love and, in that state of deep concentration, pronounce the second mantra. You will be happy, and the person you love will be happy at the same time. These mantras can be practiced in daily life. To be a true lover, you have to practice mindful breathing in order to produce your true presence.

There is a third mantra: "Darling, I know you are suffering. That is why I am here for you." If you are mindful, you will notice when your beloved is suffering. Sit close to him and say, "Darling, I know you are suffering. That is why I am here for you." That alone will bring a lot of relief.

There is a fourth mantra you can practice when you yourself suffer: "Darling, I am suffering. Please help." Only six words, but sometimes they are difficult to say because of the pride in our hearts, especially if it was the person we love whom we believe caused us to suffer. If it had been someone else, it would not be so hard. But because it was him, we feel deeply hurt. We want to go to our room and weep. But if we really love him, when we suffer like that, we have to ask for help. We must overcome our pride.

There is a story that is well-known in my country about a young couple who suffered deeply because of pride. The husband had to go off to war, and he left his pregnant wife behind. Three years later, when he was released from the army, his wife came to the village gate to welcome him, and she brought along their little boy. When the young couple saw each other, they could not hold back the tears of joy. They were thankful to their ancestors for protecting them, and the young man asked his wife to go to the marketplace to buy some fruit, flowers, and other offerings to place on the ancestors' altar.

While she was shopping, the young father asked his son to call him Daddy, but the little boy refused. "Sir, you are not my daddy! My daddy used to come every night, and my mother would talk to him and cry. When mother sat down, daddy also sat down. When mother lay down, my daddy lay down." Hearing these words, the young father's heart turned to stone.

When his wife returned, he could not even look at her. The young man offered fruit, flowers, and incense to the ancestors, made prostrations, and then rolled up the bowing mat and did not allow her to do the same. He believed that she was not worthy to present herself in front of the ancestors. Then he walked out of the house and spent his days drinking and walking about the village. His wife could not understand why he was acting like that. Finally, after three days, she could bear it no longer, and she jumped into the river and drowned herself.

The evening after the funeral, when the young father lit the kerosene lamp, his little boy shouted, "There is my daddy!" He pointed to his father's shadow projected on the wall and said, "My daddy used to come every night just like that, and my mother would talk to him and cry a lot. When my mother sat down, he sat down. When my mother lay down, he lay down." "Darling, you have been away for too long. How can I raise our child alone?" she cried to her shadow. One night the child asked her who and where his father was. She pointed to her shadow on the wall and said, "This is your father." She missed him so much.

Suddenly the young father understood, but it was too late. If he had gone to his wife and asked, "Darling, I suffer so much. Our little boy said a man used to come every night and you would talk to him and cry with him, and every time you sat down, he also sat down. Who is that person?" she would have had an opportunity to explain and avert the tragedy. But he did not because of the pride in him.

The lady behaved the same. She was deeply hurt because of her husband's behavior, but she did not ask for his help. She should have practiced the fourth mantra, "Darling, I suffer so much. Please help. I do not understand why you will not look at me or talk with me. Why didn't you allow me to prostrate before the ancestors? Have I done anything wrong?" If she had done that, her husband could have told her what the little boy said. But she did not, because she, too, was caught in pride.

In true love, there is no place for pride. When you are hurt by the person you love, when you suffer and believe that your suffering has been caused by the person you love the most, remember this story. Do not act like the father or the mother of the little boy. Do not let pride stand in your way. Practice the fourth mantra: "Darling, I am suffering. Please help." If you really consider him to be the one you love the most in this life, you have to do that. When he hears your words, he will come back to himself and practice looking deeply. Then the two of you will be able to sort things out, reconcile, and dissolve the wrong perception.

Buddhist meditation aims, first of all, at restoring communication with ourselves. We are seldom there for ourselves. We run away from ourselves, because we are afraid to go home and face the fear and suffering in our wounded child who has been ignored for such a long time. But it is wonderful to return home and say, "Little boy or little girl, I am here for you. Don't worry. I will take care of you." This is the first step. You are the deeply wounded child waiting for you to come home. And you are the one who has run away from home, who has neglected your child.

Go back and take care of yourself. Your body needs you, your feelings need you, your perceptions need you. The wounded child in you needs you. Your suffering, your blocks of pain need you. Your deepest desire needs you to acknowledge it. Go home and be there for all these things. Practice mindful walking and mindful breathing. Do everything in mindfulness so you can be really there, so you can love.

# CHAPTER SEVEN

# Deep Listening and Loving Speech

IN MANY AMERICAN UNIVERSITIES, THERE IS A COURSE CALLED Communications Skills. I am not certain what they teach, but I hope it includes the art of deep listening and loving speech. These should be practiced every day if you want to develop true communications skills. There is a saying in Vietnamese, "It doesn't cost anything to have loving speech." We only need to choose our words carefully and we can make other people very happy. The way we speak and listen can offer others joy, happiness, self-confidence, hope, trust, and enlightenment.

Never in human history have we had so many means of communication—television, radio, telephone, fax, e-mail, the worldwide web—yet we remain islands, with little real communication between family members, individuals in society, or nations. There are so many wars and conflicts. We have to find ways to open the doors of communication again. When we cannot communicate, we get sick, and we suffer and spill our suffering onto other people. We pay psychotherapists to listen to us, but psychotherapists are just human beings who have problems also.

One day in Karma Ling, a meditation center in the French Alps, I told a group of children that they should go to a friend or a parent every time they feel pain within themselves to communicate about it. Children suffer like adults. They also feel lonely, cut off, and helpless. We have to teach them how to communicate when they suffer so much.

Suppose your partner says something unkind to you, and you feel hurt. If you reply right away, you risk making the situation worse. The best practice is to breathe in and out to calm yourself, and when you are calm enough, say, "Darling, what you just said hurt me. I would like to look deeply into it, and I would like you to look deeply into it, also." Then you can make an appointment for Friday evening to look at it together. One person looking at the roots of your suffering is good, two people looking at it is better, and two people looking together is best.

I propose Friday evening for two reasons. First, you are still hurt, and if you begin discussing it now, it may be too risky. You might say things that will make the situation worse. From now until Friday evening, you can practice looking deeply into the nature of your suffering, and the other person can also. While driving the car, he might ask himself, "What is so serious? Why did she get so upset? There must be a reason." While driving, you will also have a chance to look deeply into it. Before Friday night, one or both of you may see the root of the problem and be able to tell the other and apologize. Then on Friday night, you can have a cup of tea together and enjoy each other. If you make an appointment, you will both have time to calm down and look deeply. This is the practice of meditation. Meditation is to calm ourselves and to look deeply into the nature of our suffering.

When Friday night comes, if the suffering has not been transformed, you will be able to practice the art of Avalokiteshvara—one person expressing herself, while the other person listens deeply. When you speak, you tell the deepest kind of truth, using loving speech, the kind of speech the other person can understand and accept. While listening, you know that your listening must be of a good quality to relieve the other person of his suffering. A second reason for waiting until Friday is that when you neutralize that feeling on Friday evening, you have Saturday and Sunday to enjoy being together.

Suppose you have some problem with a member of your family or community, and you don't feel joyful being with her. You can talk to her about simple things, but you don't feel comfortable talking with her about anything deep. Then one day, while you are doing housework, you notice that the other person is not sharing in the work, and you begin to feel uneasy. "Why am I doing so much and she isn't doing anything?" Because of this comparison, you lose your happiness. But instead of telling the other person, "Please, come and help with the work," you say to yourself, "Why should I have to say something to her? She should be more responsible!" You think that way because you already have some internal formation about the other person. The shortest way is always the direct way. "B" can go to "A" and say, "Sister, please come and help." But you do not do that. You keep it to yourself and blame the other person.

The next time the same thing happens, your feeling is even more intense. Your internal formation grows little by little, until you suffer so much that you need to talk about it with a third person. You are looking for sympathy in order to share the suffering. So, instead of talking directly to "A," you talk to "C." You look for "C" because you think that "C" is an ally who will agree that "A" is not behaving well at all.

If you are "C," what should you do? If you already have some internal formations concerning "A," you will probably be glad to hear that someone else feels the same way. Talking to each other may make you feel better. You are becoming allies—"B" and "C" against "A." Suddenly "B" and "C" feel close to each other, and both of you feel some distance from "A." "A" will notice that.

"A" may be very nice. She would be capable of responding directly to "B" if "B" could express her feelings to her. But "A" does not know about "B's" resentment. She just feels some kind of cooling down between herself and "B" without knowing why. She notices that "B" and "C" are becoming close, while both of them look at her coldly. So she thinks, "If they don't want me, I don't need them." She steps farther back from them, and the situation worsens. A triangle has been set up.

If I were "C," first of all, I would listen to "B" attentively, understanding that "B" needs to share her suffering. Knowing that the direct way is the shortest way, I would encourage "B" to speak directly to "A." If "B" is unable to do this, I would offer to speak to "A" on "B's" behalf, either with "B" present, or alone.

But, most important, I would not transmit to anyone else what "B" tells me in confidence. If I am not mindful, I may tell others what I now know about "B's" feelings, and soon the family or the community will be a mess. If I do these things—encourage "B" to speak directly with "A" or speak with "A" on "B's" behalf, and not tell anyone else what "B" has told me—I will be able to break the triangle. This may help solve the problem, and bring peace and joy back into the family, the community, and the society.

If, in the community, you see that someone is having difficulty with someone else, you have to help right away. The longer things drag on, the more difficult they are to solve. The best way to help is to practice mindful speech and deep listening. Good communication can bring peace, understanding, and happiness to people.

Speech can be constructive or destructive. When someone says, "I love you," it may be a lie. It may just be an expression of desire. We have to be attentive. In the Buddhist tradition, Right Speech is described as refraining from these four actions: (1) Not telling the truth. If it's black, you say it's white. (2) Exaggerating. You make something up, or describe something as more beautiful than it actually is, or as ugly when it is not so ugly. (3) Forked tongue. You go to one person and say one thing and then you go to another person and say the opposite. (4) Filthy language. You insult or abuse people.

The heart of Buddhist meditation is mindfulness. Mindfulness can help us to restore communication, first of all within ourselves. Sometimes we hate ourselves. We are afraid of ourselves. We are alienated from ourselves. We cannot communicate with ourselves. Four hundred years ago in Vietnam, there was a student who was not happy at all. He was a handsome young man, but he could not communicate with his parents, his sisters, or his brothers, and he felt completely cut off from his family. His name was Tu Uyen, but let us call him David. He was extremely lonely, and he suffered a lot. Many people had tried to befriend David, but he was so angry—filled with pain, fear, and distrust—that eventually all of them left. He did not believe in people or in happiness. He just lived alone in a small room on the university campus.

One morning he went to a Buddhist temple, hoping he might meet someone there, to make a new friend. When he arrived at the temple, he saw a group of young people going out the gate, and among them was a very beautiful young lady. He knew she was the one! He had a deep desire to have her as his friend. There was a lot of good will in his heart. So, instead of going into the temple, he followed the group of young people, but the pretty young woman just vanished.

He could not forget her beauty. Day after day he thought about her. He could not get her out of his mind. Then one night in a dream, an old man told him there was a way for him to see the young lady again. He told the young man to go to the East Market early the next morning and look deeply for her. The young man jumped out of bed and waited for the sun to rise so he could go to the East Market. When he arrived there, it was still quite early, so he went to the bookshop to buy some books for his studies. When he entered the bookshop, he looked up at a painting on the wall and saw the same young lady he had seen at the temple gate. She had the same face, the same eyes, and the same smile. So, instead of buying books, he bought the painting and brought it home. He hung it on the wall and just sat and talked to the young lady in the painting. At noon every day, he prepared a bowl of instant noodles for lunch. He put the noodles into a bowl, poured hot water over them, and waited for a few minutes. That was all. He ate plain instant noodles day after day, meal after meal, without even adding vegetables. His life was without flavor.

When you are lonely, you might talk to a tree, a rock, a cat, or a dog. It can be easier to live with a cat than with a human being, because when you say something unkind to your cat, it will not shout back at you. In the same way David would look at the painting for hours and talk to the young lady in it.

One day he decided to prepare two bowls of instant noodles. He put two pairs of chopsticks on the table, and continued to talk to the young lady. For a second, he had the impression she was smiling at him, but when he looked up again, she wasn't. Then, halfway through his bowl of instant noodles, he just stopped eating. The food was tasteless. His life was without meaning. He looked up again, and this time he was sure that she was smiling at him. Then, suddenly, she stepped down from the painting and said to him, "How can you eat noodles this way?" Then she disappeared. A moment later she reappeared with a bag filled with fresh vegetables, and in no time at all she had prepared two delicious bowls of noodles with onions, black pepper, and many fresh vegetables. You cannot imagine the young man's happiness. A wonderful friend had entered his life! She was an angel, and she told him that her name was Angelina (in Vietnamese, *Giáng Kiều*).

But the young man had so much pain in him, he did not know how to communicate. He loved her, but when she offered him advice, he did not know how to listen. He also did not know how to speak with loving kindness. He drank a lot of alcohol every day, and when he was drunk, he behaved in a most unkind way. When you have so much anger and suffering in yourself, you want to cover up your pain, and you might use alcohol or drugs to try to forget. We cannot exactly blame David. It was difficult for him to bear so much pain and anguish. No one had taught him the way of mindful living—breathing, walking, embracing his pain to transform it. Finally Angelina had to leave him. It was impossible to live with someone so full of anger, so full of pain, unable to listen or communicate.

When David realized that she was gone, he suffered so much that he wanted to kill himself. He was preparing to commit suicide, when suddenly he remembered something Angelina had told him. One beautiful morning, she had taken him to the same Buddhist temple where he had first seen her, and that morning the monk of the temple gave a Dharma talk on communicating with incense. Angelina said, "In the future, David, if you need me, if you want me to be with you, use incense to communicate." David ran to the market, bought a package of incense, and burned it right away, not just one stick but ten sticks at the same time! He sat very still and waited. More than an hour had passed, and Angelina was still not there. He was close to despair, when he remembered something else the monk had said during the Dharma talk. He had spoken of incense of the heart. He said there are five kinds of heart incense: the incense of mindfulness trainings, concentration, insight, liberation, and the flower of liberation. He realized that unless he learned how to use the incense of the heart, he could not communicate with Angelina.

The first is incense of mindfulness trainings. The fourth of the Five Mindfulness Trainings is about communication—practicing loving speech and deep listening. Unless we practice deep listening and loving speech, we cannot communicate with people. Sitting there, his life flashed before him. He saw that he had never really communicated with anyone—his father or mother, his sisters or brothers, his friends, or even Angelina. He knew that he was not practicing the fourth mindfulness training. At that moment he had an insight. He stopped blaming his parents for his suffering. He realized that he himself was responsible for it, that he had not listened or spoken mindfully, and that he had hurt others. He accepted his part of the responsibility. The moment David had that insight, he was released from his anger, and his heart began to open. He continued sitting like that for half an hour, and suddenly Angelina appeared. Angelina always has love in her heart. If you know how to begin anew, Angelina will always forgive you and come back. She will step down from the painting into your life. Each of us has several Angelinas, and we have to look deeply at the way we treat her. How do we talk to her? How do we treat her? Do we make her suffer? These are questions to reflect on.

In Plum Village there is a twenty-year-old novice monk named Phâp Canh, True Dharma Mirror. He has been practicing as a monk for only one year and four months, but he practices well and makes his Dharma brothers and sisters very happy. Brother Phâp Canh is my attendant—his task is to bring me breakfast in the morning and, if I have to go anywhere, to drive me in a small black car. He is a very mindful driver. When he gets into the car, he always practices breathing in and out while reciting the verse: "Before starting the car, I know where I am going. The car and I are one. If the car goes fast, I'll go fast." I always feel happy being with him. The communication between us is perfect.

Every morning we eat breakfast silently together, teacher and student. One morning I told him the story of David and Angelina. He was pleased to hear this story. Then I looked at him mindfully and said, "True Dharma Mirror, you are my Angelina. You have stepped into my life and made me so happy. I vow to lead my daily life in a way that you will never leave me." I saw that he was deeply moved. It was a statement of true love. But he said, "Thây, I cannot make instant noodles as well as Angelina." I continued to smile and I said, "My child, you don't have to be an excellent noodle maker to make me happy. You have many sisters in the Dharma who make noodles very well. You only need to drive me the way you drive me. That is more than enough to make me happy." He was pleased to hear that.

In my hermitage, there is a small meditation hall where I have hung a picture of all my Angelinas, one hundred of them who have stepped down from a painting and entered my life, fifty monks and nuns and fifty laypeople who live as a family in Plum Village. We practice walking meditation, sitting meditation, mindful eating, mindful movements, the bell of mindfulness, and the peace treaty. The peace treaty is about communication, anger, and listening deeply to preserve our happiness and harmony.[1]

Every night at ten o'clock, I practice the Three Prostrations. I begin by sitting down and burning a stick of incense to communicate with my ancestors. When the bell announces sitting time, I stop whatever I am doing and walk in the style of walking meditation. I don't need to wait until I get into the meditation hall to start meditating. I begin where I am, walking mindfully. Then I sit down in front of the altar. The altar at my hermitage has statues of the Buddha, bodhisattvas, and also one of Jesus Christ. I consider Jesus one of my spiritual ancestors. I sit down and take out one stick of incense. Although a stick of incense is very light, I hold it with two hands, because my practice is to do everything mindfully, to invest one hundred percent of myself into each thing I do. When you practice walking

---

[1] See pp. 119–121.

meditation, take one step at a time and take it with all your being, not just fifty percent. For it to be a real step, body and mind have to be together. I strike a match and light the tip of the incense, and I touch my ancestors. I become one with my ancestors.

We are a part of a stream of life, and when we offer a stick of incense like that, we know we are in touch with our ancestors. They are not just on the altar. They are in me, also. I am a continuation of my ancestors—my blood ancestors and my spiritual ancestors. When you can communicate with your ancestors, you are no longer lonely. Every day when I burn a stick of incense to offer to my ancestors, I look at the pictures of my grandmother, my grandfather, and all my spiritual ancestors—my teacher, the Buddha, Jesus. When I touch any of them deeply, I touch all my ancestors. When you dust your altar, you are already touching your ancestors. This is a very important daily practice for me.

In Asia, we burn incense every day and practice communicating with our ancestors. We do not feel cut off from the stream of our ancestors or from our children and their children. We are all part of the same stream of life. After I offer the stick of incense to the altar, I sit there and practice mindful breathing, contemplating the incense smoke rising. My heart is calm, and I feel in communication with everyone. I stay in that position for several minutes, sometimes longer, then I open my eyes, stand up, and bow to all my Angelinas, before sitting down to meditate. When I do this, I have the real impression all of them are sitting with me.

After Angelina returned, David was finally able to listen to her. Angelina really became his Dharma sister, and they practiced very well together and had a lot of happiness. After a few months, they decided to go to a nearby practice center. They knew that practicing in a Sangha would be easier and more effective, so they decided to go to the center and practice for a few years, to transform the pain and suffering within themselves, so they could help others release their suffering and restore their peace, their happiness, and their ability to communicate again.

Loving speech is an important aspect of practice. We say only loving things. We say the truth in a loving way, with nonviolence. This can only be done when we are calm. When we are irritated, we may say things that are destructive. So when we feel irritated, we should refrain from saying anything. We can just breathe. If we need to, we can practice walking meditation in the fresh air, looking at the trees, the clouds, the river. Once we have returned to our calmness, our serenity, we are capable again of using the language of loving kindness. If, while we are speaking, the feeling of irritation comes up again, we can stop and breathe. This is the practice of mindfulness.

The practice of Avalokiteshvara Bodhisattva is to listen very deeply to every kind of sound, including the sound of pain from within and from without. Listening to the bell, the wind, the water, the insects, and all living beings is part of our practice. When we know how to listen deeply and how to breathe deeply in mindfulness, everything becomes clear and deep.

# CHAPTER EIGHT

# *Living Mindfully Together*

THINK ABOUT YOUR FIRST LOVE, HOW IT CAME ABOUT, WHERE IT took place, what brought you to that moment. Recall the details of the experience and look at them calmly and deeply, with compassion and understanding. You will discover things you did not notice the first time. You will discover that your "first love" was not really the first. Many streams nourish and support the river of your life. Your first love has no beginning and no end; it is always in transformation. Your first love is still present, continuing to shape your life. When you are serene, smiling, and breathing mindfully, I am sure you will understand.

Where is the self? Where is the non-self? Who is your first love? Who is the last? What is the difference between your first love and your last love? Whether water is overflowing or evaporating depends on the season. Whether it is round or square depends on the container. Flowing in spring, solid in winter, its immensity cannot be measured, its source cannot be found. In an emerald creek, water hides a dragon king. In a cold pond, it contains the bright full moon. On the bodhisattva's willow branch, it sprays the nectar of compassion. One drop is enough to purify and transform the world in ten directions. Can you grasp water through form? Can you trace it to its source? Do you know where it will end? It is the same with your first love. Your first love has no beginning and will have no end. It is still alive in the stream of your being. Don't think it was only in the past. Look deeply into the nature of your first love, and you will see the Buddha.

The practice of mindfulness is the practice of love. It is important to learn the art of mindful living before entering any new relationship, especially the journey of mutual discovery that takes place in a marriage. If you do not come to know yourselves well, practicing looking deeply in order to discover all the flowers and all the garbage that are in you—not just those of your own making but those you received from your ancestors and from society—your marriage will be difficult.

When you enter a relationship, you feel excitement, enthusiasm, and the willingness to explore. But you may not really understand yourself or the other person very well yet. Living together twenty-four hours a day, you see, hear, and experience many things you have not seen or imagined before. When you fell in love, you constructed a beautiful image that you projected onto your partner, and now you are a little shocked as your illusions disappear and you discover the reality. Unless you know how to practice mindfulness together, looking deeply into yourself and your partner, you may find it difficult to sustain your love through this period.

In Buddhist psychology, the word *samyojana* refers to internal formations, fetters, or knots. When someone says something unkind to us, for example, if we do not understand why he said it and we become irritated, a knot will be tied in us. The lack of understanding is the basis for every internal knot. It is difficult for our mind to accept that it has negative feelings like anger, fear, and regret, so it finds ways to bury these in remote areas of our consciousness. We create elaborate defense mechanisms to deny their existence, but these problematic feelings are always trying to surface. If we practice mindfulness, we can learn the skill of recognizing a knot the moment it is tied in us and finding ways to untie it. Internal formations need our full attention as soon as they form, while they are still loosely tied, so that the work of untying them will be easy. Otherwise, they will grow tighter and stronger.

The first step in dealing with unconscious internal formations is to try to bring them into awareness. We meditate, practicing conscious breathing to gain access to them. They might reveal themselves as images, feelings, thoughts, words, or actions. We may notice a feeling of anxiety and ask, "Why did I feel so uncomfortable when she said that?" or "Why do I keep doing that?" or "Why did I hate that character in the movie so much?" Observing ourselves closely can bring an internal formation into view. And as we shine the light of our mindfulness on it, it begins to reveal its face. We may feel some resistance to continuing to look at it, but if we have developed the capacity to sit still and observe our feelings, the source of the knot will slowly reveal itself and give us an idea how to untie it. Practicing like this, we come to know our internal formations, and we make peace with ourselves.

When we live with another person, it is important to practice this way. To protect each other's happiness, we must learn to transform the internal formations we produce together as soon as they arise. One woman told me that three days after her wedding, she received several large internal formations from her husband, and she kept them to herself for thirty years. She was afraid that if she told him, there would be a fight. How can we be happy like that, with no real communication? When we are not mindful in our daily life, we plant the seeds of suffering in the very person we love.

But when both partners are still light and not filled with too many knots, the practice is not difficult. Together we look at the misunderstanding that created the knot, and then we untie it. For example, if we hear our husband exaggerating to his friends about something he did, we may feel a knot being tied inside us in the form of some disrespect for him. But if we discuss it with him right away, the two of us can come to a clear understanding, and the knot will be untied easily.

If we practice the art of mindful living together, we can do this. We see that the other person, like us, has both flowers and garbage inside, and we accept this. Our practice is to water the flower in her, and not bring her more garbage. We avoid blaming and arguing. When we try to grow flowers, if the flowers do not grow well, we do not blame or argue with them. We blame ourselves for not taking care of them well. Our partner is a flower. If we take care of her well, she will grow beautifully. If we take care of her poorly, she will wither. To help a flower grow well, we must understand her nature. How much water does she need? How much sunshine? We look deeply into ourselves to see our true nature, and we look into the other person to see her nature.

In the Buddhist tradition, we speak of the oneness of body and mind. Whatever happens to the body also happens to the mind. The sanity of the body is the sanity of the mind; the violation of the body is the violation of the mind. When we are angry, we may think that we are angry in our feelings, not in our body, but that is not true. When we love someone, we want to be close to him or her physically, but when we are angry at someone, we don't want to touch or be touched by that person. We cannot say that body and mind are separate.

A sexual relationship may be an act of deep communion between body and spirit. This is a very important encounter, not to be done in a casual manner. You know that in your soul there are certain areas—memories, pain, secrets—that are private, that you would only share with the person you love and trust the most. You do not open your heart and show it to just anyone. In the Imperial City, there is a zone you cannot approach called the Forbidden City; only the king and his family are permitted to circulate there. There is a place in your soul like that that you do not allow anyone to approach except the one you love and trust the most.

The same is true of our body. Our bodies have areas that we do not want anyone to touch or approach unless he or she is the one we respect, trust, and love the most. When we are approached casually or carelessly, with an attitude that is less than tender, we feel insulted in our body and soul. Someone who approaches us with respect, tenderness, and utmost care is offering us deep communication, deep communion. It is only in that case that we will not feel hurt, misused, or abused, even a little. This cannot be attained unless there is true love and commitment. Casual sex cannot be described as love. Love is deep, beautiful, and whole. In sexual relationships, respect is one of the most important elements. Sexual communion should be like a rite, a ritual performed in mindfulness with great respect, care, and love. If you are motivated by some desire, that is not love. Desire is not love. Love is something much more responsible. It has care in it.

In Asia, we say there are three sources of energy—sexual, breath, and spirit *(jing, qi,* and *shen).* Jing, sexual energy, is the first. When you have more sexual energy than you need, there is an imbalance in your body and in your being, and you need to reestablish the balance. According to Taoism and Buddhism, there are practices to help you do this, including meditation and martial arts. The second source of energy is qi, breath energy. Life can be described as a process of burning. In order to burn, every cell in our body needs nutrition and oxygen. In his *Fire Sermon,* the Buddha said, "The eyes are burning, the nose is burning, the body is burning." In our daily lives, we have to cultivate our energy by practicing proper breathing. We benefit from the air and its oxygen, so we have to be sure that nonpolluted air is available to us. Some people cultivate their qi by refraining from smoking and talking, or by practicing conscious breathing after talking a lot. When you speak, take the time to breathe. At Plum Village, every time we hear the bell of mindfulness, everyone stops what they are doing and breathes consciously three times. We practice this way to cultivate and preserve our qi energy.

The third source of energy is shen, spirit energy. When you don't sleep at night or when you worry a lot, you lose some of this kind of energy. Your nervous system becomes exhausted and you cannot study or practice meditation well, or make good decisions. You don't have a clear mind because of lack of sleep or from worrying too much. Worry and anxiety drain this source of energy. So don't worry. Don't stay up too late. Keep your nervous system healthy. Prevent anxiety. These kinds of practices cultivate the third source of energy. You need this source of energy to practice meditation well. A spiritual breakthrough requires the power of your spirit energy, which comes about through concentration and knowing how to preserve this source of energy. When you have strong spirit energy, you only have to focus it on an object, and you will have a breakthrough. If you don't have shen, the light of your concentration will not shine brightly, because the light emitted is very weak. These three sources of energy are linked to one another. By practicing one, you help all of them. That is why conscious breathing is so important for our spiritual life. It helps with all of our sources of energy.

Monks and nuns do not engage in sexual relationships because they want to devote their energy to having a break-through in their meditation practice. They learn to chan-nel their sexual energy to strengthen their spirit energy for the breakthrough. They also practice deep breathing to increase the spirit energy. Since they live alone, without a family, they can devote their time to meditation, teaching, and helping others.

In a practice community, if there is no sexual miscon-duct, there will be stability and peace. Everyone must re-spect, support, and protect each other as Dharma brothers and sisters. If someone acts irresponsibly, it creates suffer-ing in the community and in the community-at-large. If a teacher cannot refrain from sleeping with one of his or her students, he or she will destroy everything, possibly for sev-eral generations. We need mindfulness in order to have that sense of responsibility. We refrain from sexual miscon-duct because we are responsible for the well-being of so many people. If we are irresponsible, we can destroy everything. By practicing responsible behavior, we keep the Sangha beautiful.

In sexual relationships, people can get wounded. Acting responsibly prevents ourselves and others from getting hurt. We often think only women get hurt, but men also get hurt. We have to be very careful. Acting responsibly is a strong way of restoring stability and peace in ourselves, our family, and our society. We should take the time to discuss problems relating to this, like loneliness, advertising, and even the sex industry.

The feeling of loneliness is universal. There is often little communication between ourselves and others, even within the family, and our feeling of loneliness pushes us into having sexual relationships. We believe in a naive way that having a sexual relationship will make us feel less lonely, but it isn't true. When there is not enough communication with another person on the level of the heart and spirit, a sexual relationship will only widen the gap and destroy us both. Our relationship will be stormy, and we will make each other suffer. The belief that having a sexual relationship will help us feel less lonely is a kind of superstition. We should not be fooled by it. In fact, we will feel more lonely afterwards.

The union of two bodies can only be positive when there is understanding and communion on the level of the heart and the spirit. Even between husband and wife, if the communion on the level of heart and spirit does not exist, the coming together of the two bodies will only separate you further. When that is the case, I recommend that you re- frain from having sexual relationships and first try to make a breakthrough in communication.

In practicing sexual responsibility, we should always look into the nature of our love in order to see and not be fooled by our feelings. Sometimes we feel that we love another person, but that love may only be an attempt to satisfy our own egoistic needs. Maybe we have not looked deeply enough to see the needs of the other person, including the need to be safe and feel protected. If we have that kind of breakthrough, we will realize that the other person needs our protection, and therefore we cannot look upon him or her as just an object of our desire, as a kind of commercial item. Sex is used in our society as a means for selling products. If we don't look at the other person as a human being, with the capacity of becoming a Buddha, we risk transgressing the mindfulness training on sexual responsibility. The practice of looking deeply into the nature of our love is very important.

Suchness *(tathata)* is a technical term in Buddhism that means "true nature." Everything has its suchness; that is how we recognize it. An orange has its suchness; that is why we don't confuse it with a lemon. At Plum Village, we cook with propane gas, and we know its suchness. We know that if it leaks and someone lights a match, it can be very dangerous. But we also know that propane can help us cook a wonderful meal, and that is why we invite it into our house to live peacefully with us. Each of us has our own suchness. If we want to live in peace and happiness with another person, we have to understand his or her suchness and our own. Once we see it, we will have no trouble living peacefully and happily together.

To meditate is to look deeply into the nature of things, including our own nature and the nature of the person in front of us. When we see the true nature of that person, we discover his or her difficulties, aspirations, suffering, and anxieties. We can sit down, hold our partner's hand, look deeply at him, and say, "Darling, do I understand you enough? Do I water your seeds of suffering? Do I water your seeds of joy? Please tell me how I can love you better." If we say this from the bottom of our heart, he may begin to cry, and that is a good sign. It means the door of communication may be opening again.

True love includes the sense of responsibility, accepting the other person as he is, with all his strengths and weaknesses. If we like only the best things in the person, that is not love. We have to accept his weaknesses and bring our patience, understanding, and energy to help him transform. The expression "long-term commitment" helps us understand the word love. In the context of true love, commitment can only be long-term. "I want to love you. I want to help you. I want to care for you. I want you to be happy. I want to work for happiness. But just for a few days." Does this make sense? We are afraid to make a commitment. We want freedom. But we have to make a long-term commitment to love our son deeply and help him through the journey of life as long as we are alive. We can't just say, "I don't love you anymore." When we have a good friend, we also make a long-term commitment. We need her. How much more so with someone who wants to share our life, our soul, our body. The phrase "long-term commitment" cannot express the depth of love, but we have to say something so that people understand.

Your strong feelings for each other are very important, but they are not enough to sustain your happiness. Without other elements, what you describe as love may turn sour very soon. We need the support of friends and other people. That is why we have a wedding ceremony. The two families join together with other friends to witness the fact that you have come together to live as a couple. The priest and the marriage license are just symbols. What is important is that your commitment is witnessed by friends and both of your families. Now you will be supported by them. A long-term commitment is stronger and more long-lasting if made in the context of a Sangha.

The support of friends and family coming together weaves a kind of web. The strength of your feelings is only one of the strands of that web. Supported by many elements, the couple will be solid, like a tree. To be strong, a tree sends more than one root deep into the soil. If a tree has only one root, it may be blown over by the wind. The life of a couple also needs to be supported by many elements—families, friends, ideals, practice, and Sangha.

In Plum Village, every time we have a wedding ceremony, the whole community celebrates and brings its support to the couple. After the ceremony, on every full moon day, the couple recites the Five Awarenesses together, remembering that friends everywhere are supporting their relationship. Whether or not your relationship is bound by law, it will be stronger and more long-lasting if made in the presence of a Sangha—friends who love you and want to support you in the spirit of understanding and love.

Before two people marry, they should practice mindfulness together, and after becoming husband and wife, they should continue to practice the Five Awarenesses as a manifestation of their practice of mindfulness:

*We are aware that all generations of our ancestors and all future generations are present in us.*

*We are aware of the expectations that our ancestors, our children, and their children have of us.*

*We are aware that our joy, peace, freedom, and harmony are the joy, peace, freedom, and harmony of our ancestors, our children, and their children.*

*We are aware that understanding is the very foundation of love.*

*We are aware that blaming and arguing never help us and only create a wider gap between us, that only understanding, trust, and love can help us change and grow.*

In the first awareness, we see ourselves as one element in a continuation of our ancestors and as the link to future generations. When we see in this way, we know that by taking good care of our body and consciousness in the present moment, we are taking care of all generations past and future.

The second awareness reminds us that our ancestors have expectations of us and that our children and their children do too. Our happiness is their happiness; our suffering is their suffering. If we look deeply, we will know what our children and grandchildren expect of us. We may not see them in person yet, but they are already talking to us. They want us to live in a way that they won't be miserable when they manifest. Vietnamese Buddhists see themselves not as individuals, separated from their ancestors, but as a continuation representing all previous generations. Actions of the couple do not aim merely at satisfying the spiritual and physical needs of their individual selves, but also at realizing the hopes and expectations of their ancestors and at preparing for future generations.

The third awareness tells us how joy, peace, freedom, and harmony are not individual matters. We have to live in ways that allow our ancestors in us to be liberated, which means to liberate ourselves. If we do not liberate them, we ourselves will be bound all our lives, and we will transmit that to our children and grandchildren. Now is the time to liberate our parents and ancestors in us. We can offer them joy, peace, freedom, and harmony, at the same time as we offer joy, peace, freedom, and harmony to ourselves, our children, and their children. This reflects the teaching of interbeing. As long as our ancestors in us are still suffering, we cannot really be happy. If we take one step mindfully, freely, happily touching the Earth, we do it for all our ancestors and all future generations. The first three awarenesses are all aspects of one deep teaching. We have to continue to study and practice these first three awarenesses to deepen our understanding.

The fourth awareness is also a basic teaching of the Buddha. Where there is understanding, there is love. When we understand the suffering of someone, we are motivated to help, and the energies of love and compassion are released. Whatever we do in this spirit will be for the happiness and liberation of the person we love. But, sometimes we destroy the person we love. It is like the American general who said that his fighter bombers had to destroy the city of Ben Tre in order to save it. We have to practice in a way that whatever we do for others will only make them happy. The willingness to love is not enough. When people do not understand each other, it is impossible for them to love each other.

When we marry, we form a Sangha of two in order to practice love—taking care of each other, making our partner blossom like a flower, and making happiness something real. Happiness is not an individual matter. You should practice smiling at least once a day, not for yourself alone but for her also. You should practice walking meditation, not just for her, but for you also. We are linked to many other people and beings. Each step we take, each smile we make has an effect on everyone around us. Your happiness is the happiness of so many people.

Look at an oak tree. The oak tree seems to be happy, and the happiness of the oak tree is the happiness of the birds and all of us. We all benefit from its presence. Your presence and your happiness are also crucial for all of us. If you are happy, we are happy. If you are not happy, we will not be happy. You practice the Five Awarenesses not only for yourselves but for everyone. If you practice deeply the vows you made during your wedding ceremony, the whole world will profit. But to help you realize your vows, you need a community—the oak tree, the Sangha, and all of us.

"Through my love for you, I want to express my love for the whole cosmos, the whole of humanity, and all beings. By living with you, I want to learn to love everyone and all species. If I succeed in loving you, I will be able to love everyone and all species on Earth." This is the real message of love. How can we take big steps before we succeed in taking small steps? In the first one, two, or three years, this should be our purpose—to realize peace, happiness, and joy in that small Sangha. At the same time, we see our small Sangha in the context of the larger Sangha. We are practicing with the help of our teachers, parents, friends, and all living beings in the animal, vegetable, and mineral worlds. "l express my love to the larger Sangha through you. Therefore I must be able to love you, take care of you, and make you happy."

Remember to practice in the context of a community. Do whatever you can to bring happiness to the air, the water, the rocks, the trees, the birds, the humans. If you practice in this spirit, your wedding ring will become the ring of interbeing, of solidarity, of love and understanding. Live your daily life so you feel the presence of the community with you all the time. Touch the Buddha, the Dharma, and the Sangha within your heart, and you will receive the kind of energy you need every time you confront difficulties in your life and the life of the world. The world needs you to be mindful, to be aware of what is going on. Your coming together is an occasion for you to practice more deeply, and to get the support you need.

Each moment of our lives, each moment that is given to us to live, we have to live very deeply. If you are capable of living deeply one moment of your life, you can learn to live the same way all the other moments of your life. The French poet René Char said, "If you can dwell in one moment, you will discover eternity." Make each moment an occasion to live deeply, happily, in peace. Each moment is a chance for us to make peace with the world, to make peace possible for the world, to make happiness possible for the world. The world needs our happiness. The practice of mindful living can be described as the practice of happiness, the practice of love. The capacity of being happy, the capacity of being loving, is what we have to cultivate in our lives. Understanding is the very foundation of love. And looking deeply is the basic practice.

Everyone knows that blaming and arguing never help, but we forget. That is why we practice the fifth awareness. Conscious breathing helps us develop the ability to stop at that crucial moment, to keep ourselves from blaming and arguing.

All of us need to change for the better. When we marry, we make a promise to change ourselves and to help the other person change himself or herself so we can grow together, sharing the fruit and progress of practice. It is our responsibility to take care of each other. We are the gardener, the one who helps the flowers grow. If we understand, the flowers will grow beautifully.

Every time the other person does something well, something in the direction of change and growth, we should congratulate her or him to show our approval. This is important. We don't take things for granted. If the other person manifests some of her talent and capacity to love and create happiness, we must be aware of it and express our appreciation. This is the way to water the seeds of happiness. We should avoid saying destructive things like, "I don't know whether you can do this" or "I doubt that you can do this." Instead, we say, "This is difficult, darling, but I have faith that you can do it." This kind of talk makes the other person stronger. This is true with children, also. We have to strengthen the self-esteem of our children. We have to appreciate and congratulate every good thing they say and do in order to help our children grow. When we are married, we can love each other in a way that encourages change and growth for the better, all the time.

For those who have been married for ten or twenty years, this kind of practice is also relevant. You can continue to live in mindfulness and continue to learn from the other person. You may have the impression that you know everything about your spouse, but it is not so. Nuclear scientists study one speck of dust for many years, and they still do not claim to understand everything about it. If a speck of dust is like that, how can a person say that he or she knows everything about the other person? Driving the car, paying attention only to your own thoughts, you just ignore your spouse. You think, "I know everything about her. There is nothing new in her anymore." That is not correct. If you treat her that way, she will die slowly. She needs your attention, your gardening, your taking care of her.

We have to learn the art of creating happiness. If during our childhood, we saw our mother or father do things that created happiness in the family, we already know what to do. But if our parents did not know how to create happiness, we may not know how to do it. So in our practice community, we try to learn the art of making people happy. The problem is not one of being wrong or right, but one of being more or less skillful. Living together is an art. Even with a lot of good will, you can still make the other person very unhappy. Good will is not enough. We need to know the art of making the other person happy. Art is the essence of life. Try to be artful in your speech and action. The substance of art is mindfulness. When you are mindful, you are more artful. This is something I have learned from the practice.

# CHAPTER NINE

# A Rose for Your Pocket

THE THOUGHT "MOTHER" CANNOT BE SEPARATED FROM THAT OF "love." Love is sweet, tender, and delicious. Without love, a child cannot flower, an adult cannot mature. Without love, we weaken, wither. The day my mother died, I made this entry in my journal: "The greatest misfortune of my life has come!" Even an old person, when he loses his mother, doesn't feel ready. He too has the impression that he is not yet ripe, that he is suddenly alone. He feels as abandoned and unhappy as a young orphan.

All songs and poems praising motherhood are beautiful, effortlessly beautiful. Even songwriters and poets without much talent seem to pour their hearts into these works, and when they are recited or sung, the performers also seem deeply moved, unless they have lost their mothers too early even to know what love for mother is. Writings extolling the virtues of motherhood have existed since the beginning of time throughout the world.

When I was a child I heard a simple poem about losing your mother, and it is still very important for me. If your mother is still alive, you may feel tenderness for her each time you read this, fearing this distant yet inevitable event.

*That year, although I was still very young*
*My mother left me,*

*And I realized*
*That I was an orphan.*
*Everyone around me was crying.*
*I suffered in silence…*
*Allowing the tears to flow,*
*I felt my pain soften.*
*Evening enveloped Mother's tomb,*
*The pagoda bell rang sweetly.*
*I realized that to lose your mother*
*Is to lose the whole universe.*

We swim in a world of tender love for many years, and, without even knowing it, we are quite happy there. Only after it is too late do we become aware of it.

People in the countryside do not understand the complicated language of city people. When people from the city say that mother is "a treasure of love," that is already too complex for them. Country people in Vietnam compare their mothers to the finest varieties of bananas or to honey, sweet rice, or sugarcane. They express their love in these simple and direct ways. For me, a mother is like a *ba huong* banana of the highest quality, like the best *nep mot* sweet rice, the most delicious *mia lau* sugarcane!

☙

There are moments after a fever when you have a bitter, flat taste in your mouth, and nothing tastes good. Only when your mother comes and tucks you in, gently pulls the covers over your chin, puts her hand on your burning forehead—is it really a hand, or is it the silk of heaven?—and gently whispers, "My poor darling!" do you feel restored, surrounded with the sweetness of maternal love. Her love is so fragrant, like a banana, like sweet rice, like sugarcane.

Father's work is enormous, as huge as a mountain. Mother's devotion is overflowing, like water from a mountain spring. Maternal love is our first taste of love, the origin of all feelings of love. Our mother is the teacher who first teaches us love, the most important subject in life. Without my mother I could never have known how to love. Thanks to her I can love my neighbors. Thanks to her I can love all living beings. Through her I acquired my first notions of understanding and compassion. Mother is the foundation of all love, and many religious traditions recognize this and pay deep honor to a maternal figure, the Virgin Mary, the goddess Kwan Yin. Hardly an infant has opened her mouth to cry without her mother already running to the cradle. Mother is a gentle and sweet spirit who makes unhappiness and worries disappear. When the word "mother" is uttered, already we feel our hearts overflowing with love. From love, the distance to belief and action is very short.

꽃

In the West, we celebrate Mother's Day in May. I am from the countryside of Vietnam, and I had never heard of this tradition. One day, I was visiting the Ginza district of Tokyo with the monk Thien An, and we were met outside a bookstore by several Japanese students who were friends of his. One discretely asked him a question, and then took a white carnation from her bag and pinned it on my robe. I was surprised and a little embarrassed. I had no idea what this gesture meant, and I didn't dare ask. I tried to act natural, thinking this must be some local custom.

When they were finished talking (I don't speak Japanese), Thien An and I went into the bookstore, and he told me that today was what is called Mother's Day. In Japan, if your mother is still alive, you wear a red flower on your pocket or your lapel, proud that you still have your mother. If she is no longer alive, you wear a white flower. I looked at the white flower on my robe and suddenly I felt so unhappy. I was as much an orphan as any other unhappy orphan; we orphans could no longer proudly wear red flowers in our buttonholes. Those who wear white flowers suffer, and their thoughts cannot avoid returning to their mothers. They cannot forget that she is no longer there. Those who wear red flowers are so happy, knowing their mothers are still alive. They can try to please her before she is gone and it is too late. I find this a beautiful custom. I propose that we do the same thing in Vietnam, and in the West as well.

Mother is a boundless source of love, an inexhaustible treasure. But unfortunately, we sometimes forget. A mother is the most beautiful gift life offers us. Those of you who still have your mother near, please don't wait for her death to say, "My God, I have lived beside my mother all these years without ever looking closely at her. Just brief glances, a few words exchanged—asking for a little pocket money or one thing or another." You cuddle up to her to get warm, you sulk, you get angry with her. You only complicate her life, causing her to worry, undermining her health, making her go to sleep late and get up early. Many mothers die young because of their children. Throughout her life we expect her to cook, wash, and clean up after us, while we think only about our grades and our careers. Our mothers no longer have time to look deeply at us, and we are too busy to look closely at them. Only when she is no longer there do we realize that we have never been conscious of having a mother.

This evening, when you return from school or work or, if you live far away, the next time you visit your mother, you may wish to go into her room and, with a calm and silent smile, sit down beside her. Without saying anything, make her stop working. Then, look at her for a long time, look at her deeply. Do this in order to see her, to realize that she is there, she is alive, beside you. Take her hand and ask her one short question to capture her attention, "Mother, do you know something?" She will be a little surprised and will probably smile when she asks you, "What, dear?" Keep looking into her eyes, smiling serenely, and say, "Do you know that I love you?" Ask this question without waiting for an answer. Even if you are thirty or forty years old, or older, ask her as the child of your mother. Your mother and you will be happy, conscious of living in eternal love. Then tomorrow, when she leaves you, you will have no regrets.

༄

In Vietnam, on the holiday of Ullambana, we listen to stories and legends about the bodhisattva Maudgalyayana, and about filial love, the work of the father, the devotion of the mother, and the duty of the child. Everyone prays for the longevity of his or her parents, or if they are dead, for their rebirth in the heavenly Pure Land. We believe that a child without filial love is without worth. But filial devotion also arises from love itself. Without love, filial devotion is just artificial. When love is present, that is enough, and there is no need to talk of obligation. To love your mother is enough. It is not a duty, it is completely natural, like drinking when you are thirsty. Every child must have a mother, and it is totally natural to love her. The mother loves her child, and the child loves his mother. The child needs his mother, and the mother needs her child. If the mother doesn't need her child, nor the child his mother, then this is not a mother, and this is not a child. It is a misuse of the words "mother" and "child."

When I was young, one of my teachers asked me, "What do you have to do when you love your mother?" I told him, "I must obey her, help her, take care of her when she is old, and pray for her, keeping the ancestral altar when she has disappeared forever behind the mountain." Now I know that the word "What" in his question was superfluous. If you love your mother, you don't have to *do* anything. You love her; that is enough. To love your mother is not a question of morality or virtue.

Please do not think I have written this to give a lesson in morality. Loving your mother is a question of profit. A mother is like a spring of pure water, like the very finest sugarcane or honey, the best quality sweet rice. If you do not know how to profit from this, it is unfortunate for you. I simply want to bring this to your attention, to help you avoid one day complaining that there is nothing left in life for you. If a gift such as the presence of your own mother doesn't satisfy you, even if you are president of a large corporation or king of the universe, you probably will not be satisfied. I know that the Creator is not happy, for the Creator arises spontaneously and does not have the good fortune to have a mother.

I would like to tell a story. Please don't think that I am thoughtless. It could have been that my sister didn't marry, and I didn't become a monk. In any case, we both left our mother—one to lead a new life beside the man she loved, and the other to follow an ideal of life that he adored. The night my sister married, my mother worried about a thousand and one things, and didn't even seem sad. But when we sat down at the table for some light refreshments, while waiting for our in-laws to come for my sister, I saw that my mother hadn't eaten a bite. She said, "For eighteen years she has eaten with us and today is her last meal here before going to another family's home to take her meals." My sister cried, her head bowing barely above her plate, and she said, "Mama, I won't get married." But she married nonetheless. As for me, I left my mother to become a monk. To congratulate those who are firmly resolved to leave their families to become monks, one says that they are following the way of understanding, but I am not proud of it. I love my mother, but I also have an ideal, and to serve it I had to leave her—so much the worse for me.

In life, it is often necessary to make difficult choices. We cannot catch two fish at the same time, one in each hand. It is difficult, because if we accept growing up, we must accept suffering. I don't regret leaving my mother to become a monk, but I am sorry I had to make such a choice. I didn't have the chance to profit fully from this precious treasure. Each night I pray for my mother, but it is no longer possible for me to savor the excellent *ba huong* banana, the best quality *nep mot* sweet rice, and the delicious *mia lau* sugar-cane. Please don't think that I am suggesting that you not follow your career and remain home at your mother's side. I have already said I do not want to give advice or lessons in morality. I only want to remind you that a mother is like a banana, like good rice, like honey, like sugar. She is tenderness, she is love; so you, my brothers and sisters, please do not forget her. Forgetting creates an immense loss, and I hope you do not, either through ignorance or through lack of attention, have to endure such a loss. I gladly put a red flower, a rose, on your lapel so that you will be happy. That is all.

If I were to have any advice, it would be this: Tonight, when you return from school or work, or the next time you visit your mother, go into her room calmly, silently, with a smile, and sit down beside her. Without saying anything, make her stop working, and look at her for a long time. Look at her well, in order to see her well, in order to realize she is there, alive, sitting beside you. Then take her hand and ask her this short question, "Mother, do you know something?" She will be a little surprised, and will ask you, smiling, "What, dear?" Continuing to look into her eyes with a serene smile, tell her, "Do you know that I love you?" Ask her without waiting for an answer. Even if you are thirty, forty years old, or older, ask her simply, because you are the child of your mother. Your mother and you will both be happy, conscious of living in eternal love. And tomorrow when she leaves you, you will not have any regrets.

This is the refrain I give you to sing today. Brothers and sisters, please chant it, please sing it, so you will not live in indifference or forgetfulness. This red rose, I have already placed it on your lapel. Please be happy.

# CHAPTER TEN

# *Beginning Anew*

DO YOU HAVE SOMEONE TO LOVE? WE ALL WANT TO LOVE AND be loved. If you do not have anyone to love, your heart may dry up. Love brings happiness to ourselves and to the ones we love.

We may want to help those in need. We may want to love children who are hungry, disabled, or abused, to relieve them of their suffering. We carry that love in our heart and hope that someday we will be able to realize it. But when we actually contact these children, they may be difficult to love. They may be rude, they may lie, they may steal, and our love for them will fade. We had the idea that loving children who need our help would be wonderful, but when confronted with the reality, we cannot sustain our love. When we discover that the object of our love is not lovable, we feel deep disappointment, shame, and regret. We feel as though we have failed. If we cannot love a poor or disabled child, who can we love?

A number of Plum Village residents of Vietnamese origin want to go back to Vietnam to help the children and the adults there. The war created much division, hatred, and suspicion in the hearts of the people. These monks, nuns, and laypeople want to walk on their native land, embrace the people, and help relieve them of their suffering. But before they go back, they must prepare themselves. The people they want to help may not be easy to love. Real love must include those who are difficult, those who have been unkind. If they go back to Vietnam without first learning to love and understand deeply, when they find the people there being unpleasant, they will suffer and may even come to hate them.

You think you can change the world, but do not be too naive. Don't think that the moment you arrive in Vietnam, you will sit down with all the conflicting factions and establish communication immediately. You may be able to give beautiful talks about harmony, but if you are not prepared, you will not be able to put your words into practice. In Vietnam there are already people who can give very good Dharma talks, who can explain how to reconcile and live in harmony. But we should not only talk about it. If we do not practice what we preach, what can we offer anyone?

We must practice harmony of views and harmony of speech. We bring our views together to have a deeper understanding, and we use loving speech to inspire others and not hurt anyone. We practice walking together, eating together, discussing together, so we can realize love and understanding. If older sisters do not hold each other's hands like children of the same mother, how can the younger sisters have faith in the future? If you are able to breathe and smile when your sister says something unkind, that is the beginning of love. You do not have to go someplace else to serve. You can serve right where you are by practicing walking meditation, smiling, and shining your eyes of love on others.

We want to go out and share what we have learned. But if we do not practice mindful breathing to untie the knots of pain in ourselves—the knots of anger, sadness, jealousy, and irritation—what can we teach others? We must understand and practice the teachings in our daily lives. People need to hear how we have to be able to overcome our own suffering and the irritations in our own heart. When we talk about the Dharma, our words need to have energy. That is not possible if our words come only from ideas, theories, or even sutras. We can only teach what we have experienced ourselves.

Eight years ago I organized a retreat for American veterans of the Vietnam War. Many of the men and women at that retreat felt very guilty for what they had done and witnessed, and I knew I had to find a way of beginning anew that could help them transform. One veteran told me that when he was in Vietnam, he rescued a girl who had been wounded and was about to die. He pulled her into his helicopter, but he was not able to save her life. She died looking straight at him, and he has never forgotten her eyes. She had a hammock with her, because as a guerrilla, she slept in the forest at night. When she died, he kept the hammock and would not let it go. Sometimes when we suffer, we have to cling to our suffering. The hammock symbolized all his suffering, all his shame.

During the retreat, the veterans sat in a circle and spoke about their suffering, some for the first time. In a retreat for veterans, a lot of love and support is needed. Some veterans would not do walking meditation, because it reminded them too much of walking in the jungles of Vietnam, where they could step on a mine or walk into an ambush at any time. One man walked far behind the rest of us so that if anything happened he would be able to get away quickly. Veterans live in that kind of psychological environment.

On the last day of the retreat, we held a ceremony for the deceased. Each veteran wrote the names of those he or she knew had died, and placed it on an altar we constructed. I took a willow leaf and used it to sprinkle water on the names and also on the veterans. Then we did walking meditation to the lake and held a ceremony for burning the suffering. That veteran still did not want to give up his hammock, but finally he put it on the fire. It burned, and all the guilt and the suffering in his heart also burned up. We have taken one step, two steps, three steps on the path of transformation. We have to continue on that path.

Another veteran told us that almost everyone in his platoon had been killed by the guerrillas. Those who survived were so angry that they baked cookies with explosives in them and left them alongside the road. When some Vietnamese children saw them, they ate the cookies and the explosives went off. They were rolling around the ground in pain. Their parents tried to save their lives, but there was nothing they could do. That image of the children rolling on the ground, dying because of the explosives in the cookies, was so deeply ingrained on this veteran's heart, that now, twenty years later, he still could not sit in the same room with children. He was living in hell. After he had told this story, I gave him the practice of Beginning Anew.

Beginning Anew is not easy. We have to transform our hearts and our minds in very practical ways. We may feel ashamed, but shame is not enough to change our heart. I said to him, "You killed five or six children that day? Can you save the lives of five or six children today? Children everywhere in the world are dying because of war, malnutrition, and disease. You keep thinking about the five or six children that you killed in the past, but what about the children who are dying now? You still have your body, you still have your heart, you can do many things to help children who are dying in the present moment. Please give rise to your mind of love, and in the months and years that are left to you, do the work of helping children." He agreed to do it, and it has helped him transform his guilt.

Beginning Anew is not to ask for forgiveness. Beginning Anew is to change your mind and heart, to transform the ignorance that brought about wrong actions of body, speech, and mind, and to help you cultivate your mind of love. Your shame and guilt will disappear, and you will begin to experience the joy of being alive. All wrongdoings arise in the mind. It is through the mind that wrongdoings can disappear.

At Plum Village, we practice a ceremony of Beginning Anew every week. Everyone sits in a circle with a vase of fresh flowers in the center, and we follow our breathing as we wait for the facilitator to begin. The ceremony has three parts: flower watering, expressing regrets, and expressing hurts and difficulties. This practice can prevent feelings of hurt from building up over the weeks and helps make the situation safe for everyone in the community.

We begin with flower watering. When someone is ready to speak, she joins her palms and the others join their palms to show that she has the right to speak. Then she stands, walks slowly to the flower, takes the vase in her hands, and returns to her seat. When she speaks, her words reflect the freshness and beauty of the flower that is in her hand. During flower watering, each speaker acknowledges the wholesome, wonderful qualities of the others. It is not flattery; we always speak the truth. Everyone has some strong points that can be seen with awareness. No one can interrupt the person holding the flower. She is allowed as much time as she needs, and everyone else practices deep listening. When she is finished speaking, she stands up and slowly returns the vase to the center of the room.

In the second part of the ceremony, we express regrets for anything we have done to hurt others. It does not take more than one thoughtless phrase to hurt someone. The ceremony of Beginning Anew is an opportunity for us to recall some regret from earlier in the week and undo it. In the third part of the ceremony, we express ways in which others have hurt us. Loving speech is crucial. We want to heal the community, not harm it. We speak frankly, but we do not want to be destructive. Listening meditation is an important part of the practice. When we sit among a circle of friends who are all practicing deep listening, our speech becomes more beautiful and more constructive. We never blame or argue.

Compassionate listening is crucial. We listen with the willingness to relieve the suffering of the other person, not to judge or argue with her. We listen with all our attention. Even if we hear something that is not true, we continue to listen deeply so the other person can express her pain and release the tensions within herself. If we reply to her or correct her, the practice will not bear fruit. We just listen. If we need to tell the other person that her perception was not correct, we can do that a few days later, privately and calmly. Then, at the next Beginning Anew session, she may be the person who rectifies the error and we will not have to say anything. We close the ceremony with a song or by holding hands with everyone in the circle and breathing for a minute. Sometimes we end with hugging meditation.

Hugging meditation is a practice I invented. In 1966, a woman poet took me to the Atlanta Airport and then asked, "Is it all right to hug a Buddhist monk?" In my country, we are not used to expressing ourselves that way, but I thought, "I am a Zen teacher. It should be no problem for me to do that." So I said, "Why not?" and she hugged me. But I was quite stiff. While on the plane, I decided that if I wanted to work with friends in the West, I would have to learn the culture of the West, so I invented hugging meditation.

Hugging meditation is a combination of East and West. According to the practice, you have to really hug the person you are hugging. You have to make him or her very real in your arms, not just for the sake of appearances, patting him on the back to pretend you are there, but breathing consciously and hugging with all your body, spirit, and heart. Hugging meditation is a practice of mindfulness. "Breathing in, I know my dear one is in my arms, alive. Breathing out, she is so precious to me." If you breathe deeply like that, holding the person you love, the energy of care, love, and mindfulness will penetrate into that person and she will be nourished and bloom like a flower.

At a retreat for psychotherapists in Colorado, we practiced hugging meditation, and one retreatant, when he returned home to Philadelphia, hugged his wife at the airport in a way he had never hugged her before. Because of that, his wife attended our next retreat, in Chicago. To be really there, you only need to breathe mindfully, and suddenly both of you become real. It may be one of the best moments in your life.

After the Beginning Anew ceremony, everyone in the community feels light and relieved, even if we have taken only preliminary steps toward healing. We have confidence that, having begun, we can continue. This practice dates to the time of the Buddha, when communities of monks and nuns practiced Beginning Anew on the eve of every full moon and new moon. Thanks to our practice with veterans and others, we have adapted it for our community. I hope you will practice Beginning Anew in your own family every week.

Another practice you can use to bring about peace in your family and in relationships is the Peace Treaty. Because so much suffering arises when we become angry or upset, we at Plum Village drafted the Peace Treaty for couples and individuals to sign in the presence of the Sangha. The Peace Treaty is not just a piece of paper; it is a practice that can help us live long and happily together. The treaty has two parts—one for the person who is angry and one for the person who has caused the anger. I hope you will also sign and practice the Peace Treaty.

PEACE TREATY

*In Order That We May Live Long and Happily Together,*
*In Order That We May Continually Develop and Deepen*
*  Our Love and Understanding,*
*We the Undersigned, Vow to Observe and Practice the*
*  Following:*

ॐ

*I, the one who is angry, agree to:*

1. *Refrain from saying or doing anything that might cause*
   *further damage or escalate the anger.*
2. *Not suppress my anger.*
3. *Practice breathing and taking refuge in the island of*
   *myself.*
4. *Calmly, within twenty-four hours, tell the one who has*
   *made me angry about my anger and suffering, either*
   *verbally or by delivering a Peace Note.*
5. *Ask for an appointment for later in the week (e.g., Friday*
   *evening) to discuss this matter more thoroughly, either*
   *verbally or by Peace Note.*[1]

---

[1] If you feel it is not yet safe for you to speak calmly and the deadline of
twenty-four hours is approaching, you can use this "Peace Note":

Date:
Time:
Dear          ,

This morning (afternoon), you said (did) something that made me very
angry. I suffered very much. I want you to know this. You said (did):

Please let us both look at what you said (did) and examine the matter
together in a calm and open manner this Friday evening.

Yours, not very happy right now,

*I, the one who has made the other angry, agree to:*

1. *Respect the other person's feelings, not ridicule him or her, and allow enough time for him or her to calm down.*
2. *Not press for an immediate discussion.*
3. *Confirm the other person's request for a meeting, either verbally or by note, and assure him or her that I will be there.*
4. *Practice breathing and taking refuge in the island of myself to see how:*
   a. *I have seeds of unkindness and anger as well as the habit energy to make the other person unhappy.*
   b. *I have mistakenly thought that making the other person suffer would relieve my own suffering.*
   c. *by making him or her suffer, I make myself suffer.*
5. *Apologize as soon as I realize my unskillfulness and lack of mindfulness, without making any attempt to justify myself and without waiting until the Friday meeting.*
6. *Not say: "I am not angry. It's okay. I am not suffering. There is nothing to be angry about, at least not enough to make me angry."*
7. *Practice breathing and looking deeply into my daily life—while sitting, lying down, standing, and walking—in order to see:*
   a. *the ways I myself have been unskillful at times.*
   b. *how I have hurt the other person because of my own habit energy.*
   c. *how the strong seed of anger in me is the primary cause of my anger.*
   d. *how the other person's suffering, which waters the seed of my anger, is the secondary cause.*

  e. *how the other person is only seeking relief from his or her own suffering.*

  f. *that as long as the other person suffers, I cannot be truly happy.*

8. *Apologize immediately, without waiting until the Friday evening, as soon as I realize my unskillfulness and lack of mindfulness.*

9. *Postpone the Friday meeting if I do not feel calm enough to meet with the other person.*

*We Vow, with Lord Buddha as Witness and the Mindful Presence of the Sangha, to Abide by These Articles and to Practice Wholeheartedly. We Invoke the Three Gems for Protection and to Grant Us Clarity and Confidence.*

*Signed,*
*the* _____ *Day of* _____
*in the Year* _____ *in* _____ .[2]

---

[2] For a full commentary on the practice of the Peace Treaty, see *Touching Peace* (Berkeley: Parallax Press, 1992), pp. 61–71.

# CHAPTER ELEVEN

# The Five Mindfulness Trainings

*1. Aware of the suffering caused by the destruction of life,* I am committed to cultivating compassion and learning ways to protect the lives of people, animals, plants, and minerals. I am determined not to kill, not to let others kill, and not to condone any act of killing in the world, in my thinking, and in my way of life.

*2. Aware of the suffering caused by exploitation, social injustice, stealing, and oppression,* I am committed to cultivating loving kindness and learning ways to work for the well-being of people, animals, plants, and minerals. I will practice generosity by sharing my time, energy, and material resources with those who are in real need. I am determined not to steal and not to possess anything that should belong to others. I will respect the property of others, but I will prevent others from profiting from human suffering or the suffering of other species on Earth.

*3. Aware of the suffering caused by sexual misconduct,* I am committed to cultivating responsibility and learning ways to protect the safety and integrity of individuals, couples, families, and society. I am determined not to engage in sexual relations without love and a long-term commitment. To preserve the happiness of myself and others, I am determined to respect my commitments and the commitments of others. I will do everything in my power to protect children from sexual abuse and to prevent couples and families from being broken by sexual misconduct.

4. *Aware of the suffering caused by unmindful speech and the inability to listen to others,* I am committed to cultivating loving speech and deep listening in order to bring joy and happiness to others and relieve others of their suffering. Knowing that words can create happiness or suffering, I am determined to speak truthfully, with words that inspire self-confidence, joy, and hope. I will not spread news that I do not know to be certain and will not criticize or condemn things of which I am not sure. I will refrain from uttering words that can cause division or discord, or that can cause the family or the community to break. I am determined to make all efforts to reconcile and resolve all conflicts, however small.

5. *Aware of the suffering caused by unmindful consumption,* I am committed to cultivating good health, both physical and mental, for myself, my family, and my society by practicing mindful eating, drinking, and consuming. I will ingest only items that preserve peace, well-being, and joy in my body, in my consciousness, and in the collective body and consciousness of my family and society. I am determined not to use alcohol or any other intoxicant or to ingest foods or other items that contain toxins, such as certain TV programs, magazines, books, films, and conversations. I am aware that to damage my body or my consciousness with these poisons is to betray my ancestors, my parents, my society, and future generations. I will work to transform vio-

lence, fear, anger, and confusion in myself and in society by practicing a diet for myself and for society. I understand that a proper diet is crucial for self-transformation and for the transformation of society.[1]

I have been in the West for more than thirty years, and for the past fifteen I have been leading mindfulness retreats in Europe, Australia, and North America. During these retreats, my students and I have heard many stories of suffering, and we have been dismayed to learn how much of this suffering is the result of alcoholism, drug abuse, sexual abuse, and similar behaviors that have been passed down from generation to generation.

There is a deep malaise in society. When we put a young person in this society without trying to protect him, he receives violence, hatred, fear, and insecurity every day, and eventually he gets sick. Our conversations, TV programs, advertisements, newspapers, and magazines all water the seeds of suffering in young people, and in not-so-young people as well. We feel a kind of vacuum in ourselves, and we try to fill it by eating, reading, talking, smoking, drinking, watching TV, going to the movies, or even overworking. Taking refuge in these things only makes us feel

---

[1] See Thich Nhat Hanh, *For a Future To Be Possible* (Berkeley: Parallax Press, rev. ed., 1997). Until recently, I have translated the term for these as "precepts." But many Western friends told me that the word "precepts" evokes in them a strong feeling of good and evil; that if they "break" the precepts, they feel great shame. During the time of the Buddha, the word *shila* ("precepts") was usually used for these five practices, but the word *shiksha* ("trainings") was also often used. Since the meaning of the latter is more consistent with the understanding of how to practice them, without an absolute, black-and-white connotation, I have begun translating these practices as the Five Mindfulness Trainings.

hungrier and less satisfied, and we want to ingest even more. We need some guidelines, some preventive medicine, to protect ourselves, so we can become healthy again. We have to find a cure for our illness. We have to find something that is good, beautiful, and true in which we can take refuge.

When we drive a car, we are expected to observe certain rules so that we do not have an accident. Two thousand six hundred years ago, the Buddha offered certain guidelines to his lay students to help them live peaceful, wholesome, and happy lives. They were the Five Mindfulness Trainings. With mindfulness, we are aware of what is going on in our bodies, our feelings, our minds, and the world, and we avoid doing harm to ourselves and others. Mindfulness protects us, our families, and our society, and ensures a safe and happy present and a safe and happy future. The Five Mindfulness Trainings are love itself. To love is to understand, protect, and bring well-being to the object of our love. The practice of the Mindfulness Trainings accomplishes this. We protect ourselves and we protect each other.

In Buddhist circles, one of the first expressions of our desire to practice the way of understanding and love is to formally receive the Five Mindfulness Trainings from a teacher. During the ceremony, the teacher reads each Training, and then the student repeats it and vows to study, practice, and observe the Training read. It is remarkable to see the peace and happiness in someone the moment she receives the Mindfulness Trainings. Before making the decision to receive them, she may have felt confused, but with the decision to practice the Mindfulness Trainings, many bonds of attachment and confusion are cut. After the ceremony is over, you can see in her face that she has been liberated to a great extent.

When you vow to observe even one Mindfulness Training, that strong decision arising from your insight leads to real freedom and happiness. The community is there to support you and to witness the birth of your insight and determination. A Mindfulness Trainings' Transmission Ceremony has the power of cutting through, liberating, and building. After the ceremony, if you continue to practice the Mindfulness Trainings, looking deeply in order to have deeper insight concerning reality, your peace and liberation will increase. The way you practice the Mindfulness Trainings reveals the depth of your peace and the depth of your understanding and your love.

Whenever someone formally vows to study, practice, and observe the Five Mindfulness Trainings, he also takes refuge in the Three Jewels—Buddha, Dharma, and Sangha. Practicing the Five Mindfulness Trainings is a concrete expression of our appreciation and trust in these Three Jewels. The Buddha is mindfulness itself; the Dharma is the way of understanding and love; and the Sangha is the community that supports our practice.

The Five Mindfulness Trainings and the Three Jewels are worthy objects for our faith. They are not at all abstract— we can learn, practice, explore, extend, and check them against our own experience. To study and practice them will surely bring peace and happiness to ourselves, our community, and our society. We human beings need something to believe in, something that is good, beautiful, and true, something we can touch. Faith in the practice of mindfulness—in the Five Mindfulness Trainings and the

Three Jewels—is something anyone can discover, appreciate, and integrate into his or her daily life.

The Five Mindfulness Trainings and the Three Jewels have their equivalents in all spiritual traditions. They come from deep within us and practicing them helps us be more rooted in our own tradition. After you study the Five Mindfulness Trainings and the Three Jewels, I hope you will go back to your own tradition and shed light on the jewels that are already there. The Five Mindfulness Trainings are the right medicine for our time. I urge you to practice them the way they are presented at the beginning of this chapter or as they are taught in your own tradition.

What is the best way to practice the Mindfulness Trainings? I do not know. I am still learning, along with you. I appreciate the phrase that is used in the Five Mindfulness Trainings: to "learn ways." We do not know everything. But we can minimize our ignorance. Confucius said, "To know that you don't know is the beginning of knowing." I think this is the way to practice. We should be modest and open so we can learn together. We need a Sangha, a community, to support us, and we need to stay in close touch with our society to practice the Mindfulness Trainings well. Many of today's problems did not exist at the time of the Buddha. Therefore, we have to look deeply together in order to develop the insights that will help us and our children find better ways to live wholesome, happy, and healthy lives.

When someone asks, "Do you care? Do you care about me? Do you care about life? Do you care about the Earth?", the best answer is to practice the Five Mindfulness Trainings. This is to teach with your actions and not just with words. If you really care, please practice these for your own protection and for the protection of other people and species. The practice of the Mindfulness Trainings can be described as the practice of love. Because we love, because we care, because we want to protect, we practice them. They manifest our willingness to love and to protect. They are the fruit of mindfulness practice and are presented in a very concrete way. If we do our best to practice them, a future will be possible for us, our children, and their children.

# CHAPTER TWELVE

# Sangha/Community

IT IS DIFFICULT IF NOT IMPOSSIBLE TO PRACTICE THE WAY OF Understanding and Love without a Sangha, a community of friends who practice the same way. In my country, we say that if a tiger comes down from the mountain, he will be caught by humans and killed. Practicing without a Sangha is like that. Society has so much momentum in the direction of forgetfulness that we need the support of friends to help us keep in touch with our deepest desire to love and help all beings.

In the *Madhyama Agama* and *Majjhima Nikaya*, there is a sutra given by the Venerable Maudgalyayana that says: "When you practice with friends but are attached to a harmful desire, that may be the reason your friends don't speak to you and are unwilling to counsel you or teach you. Because you are caught in that harmful desire, you lose the opportunity to be taught and guided by your Sangha."[1] Maudgalyayana is counseling us to take a deep look at ourselves. He says that when we are too caught up in a strong bad habit, our friends will not be able to counsel or assist us, and we will be in difficult straits. Because we will not listen to our friends, their affection wanes, and we lose the opportunity to transform our ways.

---

[1] *Madhyama Agama* Sutra 89, *Taisho* 26, *Anumana Sutta, Majjhima Nikaya,* Sutra 15.

A Vietnamese man from Holland who visited Plum Village last year told us, "My children are not here with me because they are caught in a trap of unwholesome desires." It was not that they no longer respected or cared for their father; they had driven him all the way from Holland to Paris and helped him get on the train to Plum Village. They were just caught in a web of sorrows, and he was unable to help them out. Sometimes when we are caught in a net of unhealthy desires, we think we are on a path to happiness. According to the *Samiddhi Sutra,* such self-deception always leads to suffering. To get free of the trap of unwholesome desires, meditation and practice are needed. For us to become strong and free enough to get free or to help others, we need a loving heart, clear understanding, and great inner strength. Otherwise, we can only worry.

Every person in a Sangha needs to ask him or herself, "Am I caught in my own web of harmful desires? Am I caught in my own patterns of behavior?" This is the kind of self-examination Maudgalyayana is stressing.

In a Sangha, we always seek to find and create wholesome joys within daily life. We can't afford to love for less than twenty-four hours a day. The Four Immeasurable Minds are four *samadhis* (concentrations) that we should dwell in day and night. The Buddha's teachings need to be explored and practiced in order to illuminate how we can love each other and help people liberate themselves from painful situations.

There are many families so broken that every member is like an island. Sometimes a twelve-year-old wants to live independently of his or her family, because there is no tenderness or warmth in the family, no space to breathe. The teaching of the Four Immeasurable Minds needs to be translated into concrete practices that can be used by fathers and mothers, sons and daughters, brothers and sisters.

We need to use our understanding and love to embrace even those we consider to be our enemies. In the *Avatamsaka Sutra,* the section on Samantabhadra includes the phrase, "My only vow is to remain here in the land of utmost suffering through countless lifetimes in order to benefit all living beings." We ask the Buddhas and bodhisattvas to remain with us from lifetime to lifetime to rescue and benefit all living beings submerged in the sea of suffering. In the "Protection and Transformation Chant," we say, "Together with the Sangha, I vow to remain in this world for a long time in order to help living beings." That is the spirit of not letting go. I sometimes tell couples who want to divorce, "To divorce or not to divorce, that is not the question." The real problem lies within your own mind. Divorce may not be an option, but not divorcing may not seem an option either. You can't spit it out, and you can't swallow it.

You may think that happiness is possible only in the future, but if you learn to stop running, you will see that there are more than enough conditions for you to be happy right now. The only moment for us to be alive in is the present moment. The past is already gone and the future is not yet here. Only in the present moment can we touch life and be deeply alive. Our true home is in the here and the now. This is not difficult to understand. We only need some training to be able to do it. Practicing mindful breathing, coming back to the present moment, we can live deeply this moment and touch the wonders of life, the joy and peace that are available in the present moment.

We cannot practice deep looking unless we stop running and begin to dwell in the present moment. We do not need to run into the future to have happiness. The Kingdom of God is available here and now. We can realize this during sitting meditation, walking meditation, and sharing a meal together. We go back to the present moment and dwell there deeply, and as we train ourselves to do this, we begin to see things more deeply. There is suffering in the present moment, but there is also peace, stability, and freedom. With peace in our hearts, happiness is possible. Every kind of practice should offer us more peace, stability, and freedom. These are essential for our happiness.

We have to look with our "Sangha eyes," to know what to do and what not to do to be of help. We cannot be by ourselves alone. We can only "inter-be" with everyone else, including our ancestors and future generations. Our "self" is made only of non-self elements. Our sorrow and suffering, our joy and peace have their roots in society, nature, and those with whom we live. When we practice mindful living and deep looking, we see the truth of interbeing. I hope that Sanghas, communities of practice, will organize themselves as healthy families. We need to create environments where people can succeed in the practice. Interpersonal relationships are the key. With the support of even one person, you develop stability, and later you can reach out to others. Aware that we are seeking love, Sangha members will treat us in a way that helps us get rooted. In a spiritual family, we have a second chance to get rooted.

In the past, people lived in extended families. Our houses were surrounded by trees and hammocks, and people had time to relax together. The nuclear family is a recent invention. Besides mother and father, there are just one or two children. When the parents have a problem, the atmosphere in the home is so heavy, there is nowhere to escape, nowhere to breathe. Even if the child goes into the bathroom to hide, the heaviness pervades the bathroom. Many children today grow up with seeds of suffering. Unless we can change the situation, they will transmit those seeds to their children.

At Plum Village, children are at the center of attention. Each adult is responsible for helping the children feel happy and secure. We know that if the children are happy, the adults will be happy, too. I hope that communities of practice like this will form in the West, with the warmth and flavor of an extended family, as brothers and sisters, uncles and aunts. Our children are the children of everyone. We have to work together to find ways to help each other. If we can do that, everyone will enjoy the practice.

Nowadays, when things become difficult, couples think of divorce right away. Some people divorce many times. How can we create communities that support couples, families, single parents? How can we bring the practice community into the family and the family into the practice community?

A single mother may think she needs the support of a man, that she is not solid enough on her own. But many men are not solid in their lives either. If she enters a relationship with someone who is not solid, the stability she does have will be eroded. When a single mother comes to Plum Village to practice, we encourage her to take refuge in the island of herself. If she pursues one available man after another, she will erode her stability, and her children will grow up without a solid foundation. This is true for everyone. Don't seek for refuge in things that are not stable.

If you do, you will lose your stability. Identify your place of refuge: is it solid?

If you succeed in bringing your child up happily, you can share the fruit of your practice with many people. Parenting is a Dharma door. We need retreats and seminars to discuss the best ways to raise our children. We do not accept the ancient ways of parenting, but we have not fully developed modern ways of doing so. We need to draw on our practice and our experience to bring new dimensions to family life. Combining the nuclear family with the practice community may be a successful model. We bring our children to the practice center, and all of us benefit. If we form practice communities as extended families, the elderly will not have to live apart from the rest of society. Grandparents love to hold children in their arms and tell them fairy tales. If we can do that, everyone will be very happy.

One fourteen-year-old boy who practices at Plum Village told me this story. He said that every time he fell down and hurt himself, his father would shout at him. The boy vowed that when he grew up, he would not act that way. But one time his little sister was playing with other children and she fell off a swing and scraped her knee, and the boy became very angry. His sister's knee was bleeding and he wanted to shout at her, "How can you be so stupid! Why did you do that?" But he caught himself. Because he had been practicing breathing and mindfulness, he was able to recognize his anger and not act on it.

While the adults were taking care of his sister, washing her wound and putting a bandage on it, he walked away slowly and meditated on his anger. Suddenly he saw that he was exactly the same as his father. He told me, "I realized that if I did not do something about the anger in me, I would transmit it to my children." He saw that the seeds of his father's anger must have been transmitted by his grandparents. This was a remarkable insight for a fourteen-year-old boy. Because he had been practicing, he could see clearly like that. By making peace with our parents in us, we have a chance to make real peace with our real parents.

For those who are alienated from their families, their culture, or their society, it is sometimes difficult to practice. Even if they meditate intensively for many years, it is hard for them to be transformed as long as they remain isolated. We have to establish links with others. Buddhist practice should help us return home and accept the best things in our culture. Reconnecting with our roots, we can learn deep looking and compassionate understanding. Practice is not an individual matter. We practice with our parents, our ancestors, our children, and their children.

We have to let the ancestors in us be liberated. The moment we can offer them joy, peace, and freedom, we offer joy, peace, and freedom to ourselves, our children, and their children at the same time. Doing so, we remove all limits and discrimination and create a world in which all traditions are honored.

When we touch the present moment deeply, we also touch the past, and all the damage that was done in the past can be repaired. The way to take care of the future is also to take good care of the present moment. One Frenchwoman I know left home at the age of seventeen to live in England, because she was so angry at her mother. Thirty years later, after reading a book on Buddhism, she felt the desire to reconcile herself with her mother, and her mother felt the same. But every time the two of them met, there was a kind of explosion. Their seeds of suffering had been cultivated over many years, and there was a lot of habit energy. The willingness to make peace is not enough. We also need to practice.

I invited her to come to Plum Village to practice sitting, walking, breathing, eating, and drinking tea in mindfulness, and through that daily practice, she was able to touch the seeds of her anger. After practicing for several weeks, she wrote a letter of reconciliation to her mother. Without her mother present, it was easier to write such a letter. When her mother read it, she tasted the fruit of her daughter's practice, and peace was finally possible.

We should live our daily lives so that there is Beginning Anew in every minute. If everyone practices, there is hope for the future. Look deeply to make renewal possible. Sangha building is the most important art for us to learn. Even if we are a skilled meditator and well versed in the sutras, if we don't know how to build a Sangha, we cannot help others. We have to build a Sangha that is happy, where communication is open. We have to take care of each person, staying aware of his pain, her difficulties, his aspirations, her fears and hopes in order to make him or her comfortable and happy. This requires time, energy, and concentration.

Each of us needs a Sangha. If we don't have a good Sangha yet, we should spend our time and energy building one. If you are a psychotherapist, a doctor, a social worker, a peace worker, or if you are working for the environment, you need a Sangha. Without a Sangha, you will not have enough support, and you will burn out very soon. A psychotherapist can choose among his or her clients who have overcome their difficulties, who recognize you as a friend, a brother, or a sister in order to form a group of people to practice as a Sangha, to practice being together in peace and joy in a familial atmosphere. You need brothers and sisters in the practice in order to be nourished and supported. A Sangha can help you in difficult moments. Your capacity of helping people can be seen by looking at those around you.

I have met psychotherapists who are not happy with their families, and I doubt very much that these therapists can help us if we need them. I proposed that they form a Sangha. Among the members of this Sangha are people who have profited and recovered from their illness and have become friends with the therapist. The Sangha is to meet and practice together—breathing, living mindfully and in peace, joy, and loving kindness. That would be a source of support and comfort for the therapist. Not only do meditators and therapists have to learn the art of Sangha building, every one of us needs to. I do not believe that you can go very far without a Sangha. I am nourished by my Sangha. Any achievement that can be seen in the Sangha supports me and gives me more strength.

To build a Sangha, begin by finding one friend who would like to join you in sitting or walking meditation, precept recitation, tea meditation, or a discussion. Eventually others will ask to join, and your small group can meet weekly or monthly at someone's home. Some Sanghas even find land and move to the countryside to start a retreat center. Of course, your Sangha also includes the trees, the birds, the meditation cushion, the bell, and even the air you breathe—all the things that support you in the practice. It is a rare opportunity to be with people who practice deeply together. The Sangha is a gem.

The principle is to organize in the way that is most enjoyable for everyone. You will never find a perfect Sangha. An imperfect Sangha is good enough. Rather than complain too much about your Sangha, do your best to transform yourself into a good element of the Sangha. Accept the Sangha and build on it. When you and your family practice doing things mindfully, you are a Sangha. If you have a park near your home where you can take the children for walking meditation, the park is part of your Sangha. We begin with ourselves in order to improve the quality of our Sangha. I know the best way to improve my Sangha is to walk deeply during walking meditations, to drink my tea mindfully, to look and to touch things and people mindfully and deeply, to be more tolerant, to be more open. And that kind of practice will surely improve the quality of my Sangha. There is no other way.

A Sangha is a community of resistance, resisting the speed, violence, and unwholesome ways of living that are prevalent in our society. Mindfulness is to protect ourselves and others. A good Sangha can lead us in the direction of harmony and awareness. The substance of the practice is most important. The forms can be adapted.

Of course, our Sanghas have shortcomings. There are things around that should be improved, but the main purpose of a Sangha is to practice, to practice mindfulness, to practice being more open, tolerant, and loving. This practice will bring happiness to ourselves and to the people around us. To bring peace, happiness, and tolerance to our families, we have to practice peace, joy, and happiness with our Sangha.

Thanks to the loving support of other people, we can get in touch with the refreshing, healing elements within and around us. If we have a good community of friends, we are very fortunate. To create a good community, we first have to transform ourselves into a good element of the community. After that, we can go to another person and help him or her become an element of the community. We build our network of friends that way. We have to think of friends and community as investments, as our most important asset. They can comfort us and help us in difficult times, and they can share our joy and happiness. Even if we have a lot of money in the bank, we can die very easily from our suffering. Investing in a friend, making a friend into a real friend, building a community of friends, is a much better source of security.

Do not be afraid to love. Without love, life is impossible. We have to learn the art of loving. Love by the way you walk, the way you sit, the way you eat. Learn to love yourself and others properly. The Buddha offers us light to shine on the nature of our love. He offers very concrete ways to practice living our daily lives so love becomes something delightful. This world very much needs love. We have to help the next Buddha, Maitreya, the Buddha of love, come to be. I am more and more convinced that the next Buddha may not be just one person, but he may be a community, a community of love. We need to support each other to build a community where love is something tangible. This may be the most important thing we can do for the survival of the Earth. We have everything except love. We have to renew our way of loving. We have to really learn to love. The well-being of the world depends on us, on the way we live our daily lives, on the way we take care of the world, and on the way we love.

CHAPTER THIRTEEN

# *Touching the Earth*

IN BUDDHISM, THERE IS A PRACTICE CALLED "TOUCHING THE Earth" that can help us realize our wish to generate the energies of love, compassion, joy, and equanimity. During the practice, we touch the Earth deeply six times, surrendering ourselves to the Earth and to our own true nature. We touch the Earth with our forehead, our two legs, and our two hands, so that our mind and body form a perfect whole, allowing us to transcend our small self. We surrender our pride, notions, fears, resentments, and even our hopes, and enter the world of "things as they are." Touching the Earth is an effective yogic practice. We return to our own source of wisdom and are no longer separate and apart from our Mother Earth. The practice of love, compassion, joy, and equanimity helps establish our connectedness, which brings about health and happiness.

When I was a novice monk, I was taught this meditation:

*The one who bows and the one who is bowed to are the same.*
*When I realize this, a wondrous feeling of interbeing arises.*
*Standing on this spot with palms joined is like being held in*
*    Indra's jeweled net.*
*All Buddhas in the ten directions appear.*
*I also appear in infinite manifestations, each manifestation*
*    standing before one Buddha.*

"The one who bows and the one who is bowed to are the same." Both are without a separate self. When we look deeply into a flower, we can see the sun, the clouds, seeds, the nutrients in the soil, and many other things. We understand that the flower cannot exist as a separate, independent self. It is made entirely of what we can call "non-flower elements." The one who bows and the one who is bowed to are of the same nature. I am made of non-me elements. The Buddha is made of non-Buddha elements. Nothing can exist by itself alone. Everything has to inter-be with everything else in the cosmos.

Before bowing, we can say, "Enlightened One, you and I are of the same nature. We do not have separate selves." Do you know of any other tradition in which the faithful address the founder in this way? These are words the Buddha taught. Because we both have the nature of interbeing, our relationship is beyond expression. If I do not exist, the Buddha does not exist. If the Buddha is not, I am not. Our relationship is whole and complete.

The place where we touch the Earth is like the jeweled net of Indra. In every intersection of Indra's net is a jewel that reflects all the other jewels in the net. Looking at any one of these jewels, we see all the other jewels. Looking into a flower, we see the entire universe. All Buddhas in the ten directions appear before our eyes and also within us. In which direction should we bow? The Buddha is in front of us, and he is also behind us, to our left, our right, above, and below. Wherever the Buddha is, we are also. We join our palms and bow in the ten directions—east, west, south, north, northeast, northwest, southeast, southwest, above, and below—and also an eleventh direction: within. Bowing our heads, we respectfully bow to the Buddha, Dharma, and Sangha in the eleven directions:

> *With undivided heart*
> *to the Buddha, the Dharma, the Sangha*
> *that are in the Ten Directions*
> *and also in myself,*
> *that are in all Dharma realms*
> *transcending past, present, and future,*
> *touching the Earth and surrendering,*
> *I go for refuge with my whole body and mind.*[1]

When you touch the Earth in this spirit, isolation and alienation vanish, and your sense of a separate self will be replaced by a great feeling of oneness with all beings throughout space and time, those who have already manifested and those who have not yet manifested. This kind of bow does not diminish your personality. It restores your wholeness and connects you to the nature of awakening that is within you.

When you touch the Earth, lie close to the Earth and allow yourself to be *her,* you are absorbed into the Earth. If you practice indoors, use a mat, so you don't get dust from the floor on you. Try to remain on the Earth or the mat for at least three or four minutes. The closer you can lie against the Earth, melting into the Earth, the better. You become nothing in order to become everything.

After you have been practicing touching the Earth for two or three months, you will feel deeply refreshed, strong,

---

[1] Thich Nhat Hanh, *The Blooming of a Lotus,* p. 136 (see chap 4, n. 6).

and healthy. You will love life and be able to smile, because the energies of hatred and ill-will in you will have greatly diminished. There are six Earth-Touchings. In the first, we look deeply within. In the second, we see the connection between ourselves and other living beings, including those who live around us. By the fifth Earth-Touching, we are truly able to feel love for the people we have disliked. All of our hatred and anger will have disappeared, and we only want the person we hated to enjoy happiness and dwell in peace. We are able to reach that point because, first of all, we are able to love ourselves. Touching the Earth and reciting the six accompanying meditations generates in us deep love and acceptance. When we are able to love the person who has made us miserable, we realize what a miracle love is.

## THE FIRST EARTH-TOUCHING

*In gratitude I bow to all generations of ancestors in my blood family. I see my mother and father, whose blood, flesh, and vitality are circulating in my own veins and nourishing every cell in me. Through them, I see my four grandparents. Their expectations, experiences, and wisdom have been transmitted from so many generations of ancestors. I carry in me the life, blood, experience, wisdom, happiness, and sorrow of all generations. The suffering and all the elements that need to be transformed, I am practicing to transform. I open my heart, flesh, and bones to receive the energy of insight, love, and experience transmitted to me by all my ancestors. I see my roots in my father, my mother, my grandfathers, my grandmothers, and all my ancestors. I know I am only the continuation of this ancestral lin-*

*eage. Please support, protect, and transmit to me your*
*energy. I know wherever children and grandchildren*
*are, ancestors are there, also. I know that parents*
*always love and support their children and grand-*
*children, although they are not always able to express*
*it skillfully because of difficulties they themselves en-*
*countered. I see that my ancestors tried to build a way*
*of life based on gratitude, joy, confidence, respect, and*
*loving kindness. As a continuation of my ancestors, I*
*bow deeply and allow their energy to flow through me.*
*I ask my ancestors for their support, protection, and*
*strength.*

If you suffer like a tree cut off from its roots, it is because
you have lost touch with your family and ancestral streams.
Touching the Earth, you are able to reabsorb the vital
source of energy bequeathed to you by your ancestors.

"In gratitude I bow...." Begin by inviting the bell to
sound. At that time, you touch the Earth, and if you are
practicing with others, one person reads the meditation
while everyone bows. Remember that the words are only a
guide. You can compose words that fit your own situation.
"I see my father and mother...." As you touch the Earth,
bring your father and mother to the front of your consciousness in a concrete way, not just as an image. You are
the continuation of your parents. You *are* your parents.
Therefore, it does not make sense to be angry with your
father or mother. "Through them, I see my four grandparents...." While touching the Earth, you see your father and
mother, and through them, your paternal and maternal
grandparents. You can use photos of your grandparents
and great-grandparents, if that will help you visualize them.

Smile as you look at those photos. Understanding that your grandparents and great-grandparents are living in you gives rise to a deep feeling of connectedness and communication that is very healing.

This first Earth-Touching can be an important medicine for those who are angry at their parents or the past generations of their families. Everything you need for healing can be found within. Within you, you carry the life, blood, experience, wisdom, happiness, and sorrow of all your ancestors. You have their good health and vigor. If your great-grandfather lived to be ninety years old, you too can live that long. Why don't you follow his example? It doesn't make sense to say you'll probably die young. When you touch the Earth, speak to your great-grandfather: "Great-grandfather, please help me live a long and healthy life like you." When you link with your ancestors, you will release great stores of energy. You will be able to see their smiles and simple, healthy lifestyles. Their qualities are also in you, if you know how to bring them forth.

When you see the suffering and pain of your parents and grandparents, you know that this suffering is also present in you. Thanks to the influence of your spiritual family, you have learned to transform the pain of your parents, grandparents, and ancestors. If they were unable to accomplish certain things, you and your children can make a deep vow to fulfill those things. When you transform your own suffering, when you fulfill your own dreams, you end the suffering and fulfill the dreams of your ancestors and your descendants. You practice for all previous and future generations.

While touching the Earth, you touch all the energies of insight, love, and experience transmitted to you by your ancestors. You open yourself, not just through your mind but also through your body, to the seeds that are already in you, the energies of love, compassion, joy, and equanimity.

"I see my roots in my father, my mother, my grandfathers, my grandmothers, and all my ancestors. I know I am only the continuation of this ancestral lineage." This is the truth, not just words. The elements of stability, peace, joy, and faith that were present in your parents and ancestors are also present in you. They were transmitted to you genetically and culturally, whether or not your parents knew they were transmitting them. In Vietnam, we say, "Come here and receive your family inheritance." "Please support, protect, and transmit to me your energy." These are words of deep intention. You make a request for those energies to be shared, but in fact they are already in you.

"I know wherever children and grandchildren are, ancestors are there, also." Vietnamese culture has preserved a saying for centuries that says "wherever the grandchildren are, the grandparents are." If you are in North America, your ancestors are with you in North America, even if they never visited North America in their lifetimes. They have never died. They continue in you. Whenever you laugh, they laugh; whenever you cry, they cry. Whenever you hate, they hate; whenever you give up, they give up. That is the wisdom of the Buddha.

"I know that parents always love and support their children and grandchildren, although they are not always able to express it skillfully because of difficulties they themselves encountered." There are people who are angry at their parents because they were never able to manifest their love. But that love was still present in their store consciousness. There are no parents who do not love their children, even if to all outward appearances they hate, reject, or even try to kill their children. The love that is buried there is transmitted from one generation to the next. If parents, grandparents, and ancestors do not love and protect their children, who possibly can?

A young banana plant has only two leaves. When the third leaf appears, the first two leaves nourish the third leaf. The first two leaves have breathed air and absorbed sunshine to enable the third leaf to unfold and grow. When the fourth leaf appears, the third leaf has joined with the first two leaves to nourish the fourth. That continues until the banana tree grows large. By then, the first leaves will have begun to wither, but their energy is accumulated in all the leaves that have grown afterwards. If you look deeply at one of the recent leaves, you will see the presence of the former leaves and understand that they have never disappeared. If you look deeply into yourself, you will see all the energy of your parents, grandparents, and ancestors. If that energy has not accumulated within you, where else has it gone? To persist in hating and rejecting your parents is a useless activity. Perhaps your parents found themselves in such difficult circumstances, and they took it out on you by yelling, condemning, rejecting, and making you miserable. Even so, you cannot claim you are not their continuation or that you did not receive any nourishment or protection at all from them.

People who are angry at their parents need to look deeply and carefully at this. Westerners have been following a path of such extreme individualism for so long that many people have isolated themselves from their parents, ancestors, and society. "I see that my ancestors tried to build a way of life based on gratitude, joy, confidence, respect, and loving kindness." Look deeply to see the efforts of countless past generations. We stand on this Earth, we breathe, we see trees and flowers. In doing so, we also see all previous generations. There is no way to separate ourselves from them. Believing that we are alone or isolated is an illusion that causes much suffering. "As a continuation of my ancestors, I bow deeply and allow their energy to flow through me. I ask my ancestors for their support, protection, and strength." At this point, the bell is invited to sound and we stand up.

During the First Earth-Touching, you have been able to renew your connections with all your ancestors. After only a few weeks of practicing like that, you will feel revitalized and the sense of being alone or rejected will disappear. You will begin to feel love for your father and mother, perhaps for the first time. And you will begin to love and accept yourself.

After the First Earth-Touching, stand for five or six in- and out-breaths before beginning the second exercise. Then touch the Earth again and recite:

## THE SECOND EARTH-TOUCHING[2]

*In gratitude, I bow to all generations of ancestors in my spiritual family. I see in myself my teacher, the one who shows me the way of love and understanding, the way to breathe, smile, forgive, and live deeply in the*

---

[2] The Second Earth-Touching is to our spiritual ancestors in the Buddhist tradition. It is for anyone who appreciates the Buddha's way. In addition, we can practice the Sixth Earth-Touching (page 165) to our Judaeo-Christian spiritual roots, or compose the equivalent for our own tradition.

*present moment. I see through my teacher all teachers over many generations, all bodhisattvas, and the Buddha Shakyamuni, the one who started my spiritual family 2,600 years ago. I see the Buddha as my teacher and also as my spiritual ancestor. I see that the energy of the Buddha and of many generations of teachers has entered me and is creating peace, joy, understanding, and loving kindness in me. I know that the energy of the Buddha has deeply transformed the world. Without the Buddha and all these spiritual ancestors, I would not know the way to practice to bring peace and happiness into my life and into the lives of my family and society. I open my heart and my body to receive the energy of understanding, loving kindness, and protection from the Buddha, the Dharma, and the Sangha over many generations. I am the continuation of the Buddha, the Dharma, and the Sangha. I ask these spiritual ancestors to transmit to me their infinite source of energy, peace, stability, understanding, and love. I vow to practice to transform the suffering in myself and the world, and to transmit their energy to future generations of practitioners.*

"I see in myself my teacher, the one who shows me the way of love and understanding, the way to breathe, smile, forgive, and live deeply in the present moment." As you touch the Earth, you see your teacher, you see his or her face clearly. If he or she has already died, every morning when you light incense and breathe mindfully and look at his or her photo on the altar, don't think it's just an empty ritual. To offer incense on the Buddha's altar—the altar of your spiritual and family ancestors—is an authentic practice. Your body and mind are calm and peaceful. Holding the incense, you know that you are practicing in order to connect with your spiritual ancestors. Looking into the eyes of your teacher, you know that you are the continuation of your teacher. You see the stream of your spiritual ancestors. Perhaps your teacher has faults, but he is still your teacher, and he carries within him the wisdom of many generations.

It is very good to place photos of either your spiritual and/or your family ancestors on your altar. Even the picture of one person is helpful—the picture of someone you have encountered in this life who represents all your spiritual ancestors. Looking at his face, you have many recollections of sounds and images. Those very sounds and images can help you connect with your spiritual ancestors. You can place two or three photos on the altar, but there should be at least one. Every time you light incense at the altar, maintain mindfulness. Your eyes connect with the photo, and you smile at your teacher. "My Teacher, I light this incense for you."

"I see through my teacher all teachers over many generations." At first, you see the image of your teacher's teacher. If you can see your teacher, you can see his teacher. Without his teacher, your teacher could not be. If you have been lucky enough to live alongside your teacher's teacher for a period of time, this meditation will be easy. Sounds, images, and memories make looking deeply easier. You invite other teachers in your spiritual lineage, calling them by name. If you have studied with different spiritual elders and teachers, you will have a clearer idea who they are. You know that if they had not been, you would not be, that thanks to them, you are now learning how to breathe, smile, meditate, and transform suffering. When you recite their names and look deeply, you will naturally make contact with them, and their energy will manifest in your own blood. Even if some of those elders have faults, just as your parents and grandparents had faults, you can still accept them.

"I see the Buddha as my teacher and also as my spiritual ancestor." The Buddha is your spiritual ancestor. You can feel an intimate link with the Buddha and not think of him as some distant and removed deity, or historical figure. As a human being, you are a child of the Buddha, and he has transmitted countless precious jewels to you through your teachers and spiritual elders. See clearly that the Buddha is within you. When you can see that, you will receive the energy of the Buddha, which is mindfulness. While meditating on the Buddha, you also meditate on all the Buddha's teachers. Although their understanding was not as deep as the Buddha's, in the beginning of his practice the Buddha depended on them for guidance and support. The Buddha had roots, too. He had parents, grandparents, and teachers like all of us. The Buddha Nhien Dang (Dipankara) served as the Buddha's teacher in one of the Buddha's past incarnations and initiated him in the practice, just as Sudhana studied with fifty-three other teachers, whose number included teachers from other religions and teachers who were still quite young.

"I see that the energy of the Buddha and of many generations of teachers has entered me and is creating peace, joy, understanding, and loving kindness in me." If you contain any energy of peace, understanding, and love, it is thanks to your spiritual ancestors. Once you see that, you will be filled with their energy.

"I know that the energy of the Buddha has deeply transformed the world." Though Buddhism has been transmitted relatively recently to the West, it has already had an important impact. Buddhism was transmitted to Vietnam in the second century, and it has beautified Vietnamese spiritual life and culture in ways that have benefited the entire country. Even Vietnamese who are not Buddhist contain the essence of the Buddha in their blood. For two thousand years, the Vietnamese people have been influenced by the love, compassion, and understanding of the Buddha. It is not unusual to see an old woman in Vietnam gently pat a tree whose branch is broken. Her gentle touch has been produced by the streams of love and compassion that have penetrated the Vietnamese people for generations. Buddhism helped civilize the Vietnamese people, a fact especially easy to see during the Ly and Tran dynasties in which the spirit of Buddhism motivated all the people from emperor to commoner. For example, during the Ly dynasty, when a prisoner of war from Champa was recognized as a Buddhist teacher, he was elevated to the position of National Teacher. That was Zen Master Thao Duong. Such an event demonstrates a very open attitude.

"Without the Buddha and all these spiritual ancestors, I would not know the way to practice to bring peace and happiness into my life and into the lives of my family and society." During this Earth-touching, it is important to connect with your spiritual family. We cannot find happiness if the only family we have is our blood family. We all need two families—blood and spiritual. When you experience troubles with your blood family, your spiritual family can help; when your spiritual family is having difficulties, your blood family can offer comfort. If you lack one of these families, you will feel orphaned, and so a wise person has two. For those of you of other faiths, please also practice the Sixth Earth-Touching.

## THE THIRD EARTH-TOUCHING

*In gratitude, I bow to this land and all of the ancestors who made it available. I see that I am whole, protected, and nourished by this land and all of the living beings who have been here, and, with all their efforts, made life easy and possible for me. I see George Washington, Thomas Jefferson, Abraham Lincoln, Dorothy Day, Martin Luther King, Jr., and all the others known and unknown. I see all those who have made this country a refuge for people of so many origins and colors, by their talent, perseverance, and love, those who have worked hard to build schools, hospitals, bridges, and roads, to protect human rights, to develop science and technology, and to fight for freedom and social justice. I see myself touching my ancestors of Native American origin who have lived on this land for such a long time and known the ways to live in peace and harmony with nature, protecting the mountains, forests, animals, vegetation, and minerals of this land. I feel the energy of this land penetrating my body and soul, supporting and accepting me. I vow to cultivate and maintain this energy and transmit it to future generations. I vow to contribute my part in transforming the violence, hatred, and delusion that still lie deep in the collective consciousness of this society so that future generations will have more safety, joy, and peace. I ask this land for its protection and support.*

These are the words practitioners in the United States might use for the third Earth-Touching. Whatever country you are in, connect with the sacred land, water, and air of your country. If you are in Germany, meditate on Germany; if you are in Switzerland, meditate on Switzerland; if you are in France, meditate on France; if you are in Vietnam, meditate on Vietnam. Every land has its history of suffering and success. Wherever you live, be in touch with the air, mountains, rivers, fruits, vegetables, and grains of that land that nourish you and have played an important role in that land's history and development.

"I see that I am whole, protected, and nourished by this land and all of the living beings who have been here, and, with all their efforts, made life easy and possible for me.... I see myself touching my ancestors of Native American origin who have lived on this land for such a long time...." Americans may be white, black, brown, or yellow, but their ancestors include Indians who were the first to settle the American land. "I see George Washington, Thomas Jefferson, Abraham Lincoln, Dorothy Day, Martin Luther King, Jr., and all the others known and unknown." These are leader citizens of the United States you might remember. You might also want to mention special others. "I see all those who have made this country a refuge for people of so many origins and colors...." There are many different nationalities in the United States. In the United States, and in Vietnam, too, there are many minorities that have contributed significantly to the country's development.

"...by their talent, perseverance, and love, those who have worked hard to build schools, hospitals, bridges, and roads, to protect human rights, to develop science and technology, and to fight for freedom and social justice."

You must be able to see all these efforts. For example, when you swallow a pill that relieves a stomachache, you should be aware that the medicine did not simply fall from the sky but is the result of many generations' research. When you eat a sweet, delicious carrot, you see that it, too, is the result of many generations' efforts. A loaf of bread has a history of thousands of years behind it. In Vietnam, when we eat a bowl of noodles, we are aware that the bowl of noodles has its own history. Mothers don't know automatically how to season a bowl of noodles. That knowledge has been transmitted across many generations. Every cake, every dish has its own history. The happiness of our ancestors has become our own happiness.

In the United States, the tremendous labor of many African-Americans brought over as slaves, was responsible for cultivating the land and construction of many roads, schools, hospitals, and more. An American of European or Asian descent who is aware will see all the labor, sweat, and tears contributed by African-Americans. African-Americans are the ancestors of all Americans. It is the same in France. France does not belong only to people of French origin. In fact, it is not possible to find a person who is pure French because France is made up of many non-French elements. The French scientist Marie Curie came from Poland. The singer Yves Montand is from Italy. Our peoples, countries, and ancestors come from many different races and roots.

When you practice, you connect with all your ancestors and with the rivers, mountains, plants, and foods of your land. What are you but the manifestation and continuation of all those elements? "I feel the energy of this land penetrating my body and soul, supporting and accepting me. I vow to cultivate and maintain this energy and transmit it to future generations. I vow to contribute my part in transforming the violence, hatred, and delusion that still lie deep in the collective consciousness of this society so that future generations will have more safety, joy, and peace." Of course, we are ready to accept the positive, but we also have to accept the negative in our society, such as violence, hatred, and racism, in order to transform it. We must live in a way that contributes to the transformation of those negative elements. "I ask this land for its protection and support."

## THE FOURTH EARTH-TOUCHING

*In gratitude and compassion, I bow down and transmit my energy to those I love. All the energy I have received I now want to transmit to my father, my mother, everyone I love, all who have suffered and worried because of me and for my sake. I know I have not been mindful enough in my daily life. I also know that those who love me have had their own difficulties. They have suffered because they were not lucky enough to have an environment that encouraged their full development. I transmit my energy to my mother, my father, my brothers, my sisters, my beloved ones, my husband, my wife, my daughter, and my son, so that their pain will be relieved, so they can smile and feel the joy of being alive. I want all of them to be healthy and joyful. I know that when they are happy, I will also be happy. I no longer feel resentment towards any of them. I pray that all ancestors in my blood and spiritual families will focus their energies toward each of them, to protect and support them. I know that I am not separate from them. I am one with those I love.*

We all have people in our lives whom we especially love—
father, mother, brother, sister, son, daughter, uncle, aunt,
niece, nephew, special friends. We want these people to be
healthy and happy. We practice the fourth Earth-Touching
to transmit energy to those we love. As you touch the Earth,
you meditate as follows: "All the energy I have received I
now want to transmit to my father, my mother, everyone I
love…." Even if your father or mother has already died, you
can transmit that energy because, at the very least, your father or mother is still a part of you. Recite the name of each
one of your loved ones in both your blood and spiritual
families. You must be able to see that person's face in a very
real way—not just a passing mention. Don't lump them all
in some generic phrase, like "all those I love." Mention
each person by name—my brother Richard Warren, my sister Leslie Barton. A monk or nun can recite: "for my
teacher, my teacher's teacher, for my elder sister in the
Dharma, my elder brother in the Dharma, for all those who
practice with me in my Sangha; I wish for each one of them
to enjoy peace, joy, and happiness. For all those I encounter in my daily life, those with difficulties and those without,
may they all be happy."

"I transmit my energy to my mother, my father, my brothers, my sisters, my beloved ones, my husband, my wife, my
daughter, and my son, so that their pain will be relieved, so
they can smile and feel the joy of being alive." You want
them all to be happy, even if they have caused you sadness
or anger in the past. They are the ones you love and your
deepest desire is for their happiness.

"I pray that all ancestors in my blood and spiritual families will focus their energies toward each of them, to protect
and support them. I know that I am not separate from

them. I am one with those I love." When you touch the Earth and practice this meditation, you see that the happiness of those you love is your own, and all false boundaries disappear. This is a meditation on love. It is very easy because the object of your meditation is those you love.

### THE FIFTH EARTH-TOUCHING

*In understanding and compassion, I bow down to reconcile myself with all those who have made me suffer. I open my heart and send forth my energy of love and understanding to everyone who has made me suffer, to those who have destroyed much of my life and the lives of those I love. I know now that these people have themselves undergone a lot of suffering and that their hearts are overloaded with pain, anger, and hatred. I know that anyone who suffers that much will make those around him or her suffer. I know they may have been unlucky, never having the chance to be cared for and loved. Life and society have dealt them so many hardships. They have been wronged and abused. They have not been guided in the path of mindful living. They have accumulated wrong perceptions about life, about me, and about us. They have wronged us and the people we love. I pray to my ancestors in my blood and spiritual families to channel to these persons who have made us suffer, the energy of love and protection, so that their hearts will be able to receive the nectar of love, and blossom like a flower. I pray that they can be transformed to experience the joy of living, so that they will not continue to make themselves suffer, and make others suffer. I see their suffering and do not want to hold any feelings of hatred or anger in myself toward*

*them. I do not want them to suffer. I channel my energy*
*of love and understanding to them, and ask all my*
*ancestors to help them.*

This meditation concerns the fifth category of the five
categories of persons—persons you hate. As you touch the
Earth, meditate as follows: "I open my heart and send forth
my energy of love and understanding to everyone who has
made me suffer...." State their names and hold a clear image of their faces in your mind. See their suffering and
their anger. "I know now that these people have themselves
undergone a lot of suffering...." This is the nature of deep
looking. Meditate in order to see the roots of anger and
pain in each person you dislike. Understanding is the key
to open the heart, so this meditation is very important. You
must be able to see how the person who has made you suffer has suffered and continues to suffer himself. You need
to see what has led him to his current situation. People who
suffer make those around them suffer. "I know they may
have been unlucky, never having the chance to be cared for
and loved." Such persons have suffered from the time they
were small children. They have been wronged and abused.
Once you can see that your heart will open.

"They have not been guided in the path of mindful living. They have accumulated wrong perceptions about life,
about me, and about us. They have wronged us and the
people we love." When a person has wrong perceptions,
she suffers and causes those around her, including those
she loves, to suffer as well. "I pray to my ancestors in my
blood and spiritual families to channel to these persons
who have made us suffer, the energy of love and protection,
so that their hearts will be able to receive the nectar of love,

and blossom like a flower." You really desire that, you don't harbor ill wishes or desire that person to suffer. If that person suffers, you will also. "I pray that they can be transformed to experience the joy of living, so that they will not continue to make themselves suffer, and make others suffer." You understand that that person has not learned self-control and has therefore caused you and those you love to suffer.

You pray for all those who have caused your family and country to suffer, including murderers, thieves, profiteers, liars, and despots, to be transformed by the merits of the Buddha, bodhisattvas, and ancestors. You see how their suffering has extended throughout many generations, and you do not want to hold on to hatred and resentment. You do not want them to suffer anymore. The roots you have received from your blood and spiritual ancestors allow your heart to blossom like a flower, and you pray to let go of every feeling of hatred and resentment. You pray that everyone who has caused you, your family, or your people to suffer be released from all danger and pain in order to enjoy a life brightened with happiness, peace, and joy. You channel your energy of love and understanding to that person or persons. You ask the Buddha, bodhisattvas, and ancestors to help them.

When you really see the suffering, hardships, and wrong perceptions of a person who has made you suffer, you are able to love and forgive him. At that moment the stream of love and compassion fills your heart. Your heart is refreshed and soothed, and you are the first person to benefit from peace and joy. Afterwards, the way you live your daily life will have the capacity to transform the other person.

This is the practice of the Four Immeasurable Minds—love, compassion, joy, and equanimity.

Love your enemy as yourself. When you can love your enemy, he is no longer an enemy but a person you love. A true Buddhist has only persons he loves. There are no enemies. "Love your enemy as yourself" is a line in a song called "A Flower Has Blossomed on the Path of Our Homeland," written by Pham The My during the Vietnam War. There is a wonderful tradition in Vietnam. After a battle in which an enemy general has been killed, an altar is set up in his honor. It is a way of saying, "Though we did not want to, we were forced to kill you. Now that you are gone, we dedicate this altar to you. We know that you were following the orders of your own king. Perhaps you did not want to invade or fight us, just as we did not want to kill you, but you had no choice." The Vietnamese followed that custom for many centuries. You can see by that custom how love, compassion, joy, and equanimity penetrated the culture of Vietnam over a long period of time. I believe that in the future there will be shrines built in Vietnam to honor all the American GIs who lost their lives in Vietnam. That is our tradition.

When you practice Touching the Earth, you will enter the meditation of love, compassion, joy, and equanimity. The depth of your meditation will depend on the strength of your concentration and your ability to look deeply. Touching the Earth must be a real practice, not an act of penance or an exercise for the imagination. As your body touches the Earth, the boundaries of your individual self dissolve and you connect with your blood, spiritual, and national ancestors. You touch those you love, and you forgive those who have made you suffer. Naturally, you become healthier, lighter, and fuller. Touching the Earth has the capacity to heal, strengthen, and bring happiness. We must practice love during sitting meditation, walking meditation, and Touching the Earth. We must practice love twenty-four hours a day. Less will not do. We must know how to become a person who dwells in love, compassion, joy, and equanimity every hour of every day.

## THE SIXTH EARTH-TOUCHING

*In gratitude and compassion, I bow down to my ancient spiritual roots. I see myself as a child, sitting in church or synagogue, ready for the sermon or ceremony—Yom Kippur, Holy Communion.... I see my priest, pastor, minister, rabbi, and the people in the congregation. I remember how difficult it was to be there and to do things I did not understand or want to do. I know communication was difficult, and I did not receive much joy or nourishment from these services. I felt anxious and impatient. Because of the lack of communication and understanding between my spiritual family and me, I left my rabbi, my pastor, my synagogue, my church. I lost contact with my spiritual ancestors and became disconnected from them. Now I know there are jewels in my spiritual tradition, and that the spiritual life of my tradition has contributed greatly to the stability, joy, and peace of my ancestors for many generations. I know those who practice my spiritual tradition were unsuccessful in transmitting it to me, to us. I want to go back to them to rediscover the great spiritual values in my tradition, for my own nourishment and the nourishment of my children and their children. I want to connect again with my an-*

*cient spiritual ancestors and get their spiritual energy*
*flowing freely to me again. I see Moses, Jesus, and so*
*many others as my spiritual ancestors. I see teachers*
*over many generations in these traditions as my spiri-*
*tual ancestors, and I bow down to all of them in the*
*present moment.*

Many Westerners attracted to Buddhist practice have
abandoned their own spiritual traditions. They reject the
churches and clergy of their own traditions because they
feel constricted and uncomfortable with the attitudes and
practices they have encountered there. They have suffered
within their own tradition and so have sought another.
They approach Buddhist practice with the hope of replac-
ing their own tradition and may wish to break away from
their own tradition forever. According to Buddhist wisdom,
such wishing is in vain. A person severed from her own culture and traditions is like a tree pulled out by the roots.
Such a person will find it hard to be happy. Buddhist practice can offer effective means to heal, reconcile, and re-
unite with one's blood and spiritual families, in order to
discover the precious gems in one's own traditions. Thanks
to the practice, people will see that Buddhism and their
own spiritual tradition have many things in common, and
therefore it is not necessary to reject their own spiritual tradition. They will see that there are things that need to be
transformed in Buddhism as well as in their own tradition.

If one's spiritual or blood family lacks vitality, transformation will not be possible. It is like a tree that needs to have
certain branches pruned or else it will topple. A spiritual
tradition needs to be tended and renewed in order to remain vital. You can use the methods of Buddhist practice to

help you transform your own spiritual tradition, in order to uncover its beautiful, fine, and precious aspects. Once persons from other traditions see that Buddhist practice and their own spiritual tradition are not opposed, they will be able to enrich and illumine their own tradition and in so doing become truly happy. The same goes for Buddhists. Buddhists can appreciate the beautiful, fine, and precious things in other spiritual traditions and use them to enrich Buddhism. Buddhism has been practiced in this spirit for 2,600 years. The willingness to be enriched by other sources and to be transformed has enabled Buddhism to continually attune itself to the real needs of each generation.

Touching the Earth is an art. Do not practice in blind faith. After practicing for several weeks, take note—mentally or with pen and paper—of the reflections and intentions that arise within you, and then use that insight in your practice.

# CHAPTER FOURTEEN

# The Three Prostrations

THERE IS ANOTHER PRACTICE OF TOUCHING THE EARTH CALLED the Three Prostrations. We surrender our so-called self to the stream of life and look deeply into our nature of interbeing. Every evening in my hermitage in France, before practicing sitting meditation, I practice these Three Prostrations:

## THE FIRST PROSTRATION

*Touching the Earth, I connect with ancestors and descendants of both my spiritual and my blood families. My spiritual ancestors include the Buddha, the bodhisattvas, the noble Sangha of Buddha's disciples, [Insert names of others you would like to include], and my own spiritual teachers still alive or already passed away. They are present in me because they have transmitted to me seeds of peace, wisdom, love, and happiness. They have woken up in me my resource of understanding and compassion. When I look at my spiritual ancestors, I see those who are perfect in the practice of the precepts, understanding, and compassion, and those who are still imperfect. I accept them all because I see within myself shortcomings and weaknesses. Aware that my practice of the precepts is not always perfect, and I am not always as understanding and compassionate as I would like to be, I open my heart and accept all my spiritual descendants. Some of my descendants practice the precepts, understanding, and compassion in a way which invites confidence and respect, but there are also those who come across with many difficulties and are constantly subject to ups and downs in their practice.*

*In the same way I accept all my ancestors on my mother's side and my father's side of the family. I accept all their good qualities and their virtuous actions and I also accept all their weaknesses. I open my heart and accept all my blood descendants with their good qualities, their talents, and also their weaknesses.*

*My spiritual ancestors and my blood ancestors, my spiritual descendants and my blood descendants are all part of me. I am them and they are me. I do not have a separate self. All exist as part of a wonderful stream of life which is constantly moving.*

The First Prostration can be described as a vertical line. As we touch the Earth, we visualize first our spiritual ancestors and then our blood ancestors. During the first part of this prostration, I visualize Shakyamuni Buddha and other great teachers like Shariputra, Nagarjuna, Vasubhandu, down to my own teacher, from whom I received the ten precepts as a novice. I visualize these ancestors as perfect or nearly perfect. The original Sangha consisted of 1,250 monks. Among them some were close to perfect, but some transgressed the precepts. Some of my ancestors were nearly perfect and some were not perfect at all, but all of them are my ancestors, and I know it is important to accept them all. In myself there are also aspects that are close to perfect and things that are far from perfection. That is why I can feel peace and harmony with all my ancestors, even those who were not so perfect.

Why do we think we have the right to demand that our ancestors be perfect? In us there are also weaknesses. When we can see and accept the imperfections in ourselves, it is easy for us to accept all our ancestors, even our parents. The moment we accept them, we feel deep peace and reconciliation and see ourselves as part of the stream of life.

Next I visualize the younger generation. I see my students who are close to perfect and those who are far from perfection, and I accept them all. Some of my students have peace, solidity, freedom, and joy, and they nourish me and bring me happiness. I love them, but I also love those who have ups and downs, who have difficulties on the path, who have weaknesses, who are not at all close to perfection. Since I have weaknesses within myself, why should I not accept my students who have weaknesses? I have tolerance and acceptance for those above me in the line of time and those below me. When I visualize those who have difficulties, who do not listen to my advice, who violate the precepts, who make the Sangha unhappy, I see that the Sangha and I have to devote more time, energy, and care to those students. When you can accept everyone, your heart is filled with peace and love. Love is a process of learning, a practice, not a gift from on high.

You might like to stay in the position of prostration for five or more minutes while you visualize all these people. Call some of their names to make the practice concrete. When you touch the stream of ancestors and future generations, you become integrated into the stream of life, and you know deeply that all your ancestors and future generations are alive in you. All feelings of loneliness will disappear.

Do exactly the same for your blood family. Call the name of your grandfather or someone before him. Call your father, your mother, your aunt, your uncle. Some of them are close to perfect and others are not close to perfect at all. Some have made you very happy, and some have made you suffer. You can accept them all as your ancestors. I know that some of you do not want to have anything to do with your parents or ancestors, because you have so much anger and hatred toward them. You want to be alone and have nothing to do with them. But that is impossible. If you look deeply into yourself, you will see that you are a continuation of them, the things that are close to perfect, and the things that are very far from being perfect. You are not an isolated identity. You are part of the stream of life. This is the practice of interbeing, of non-self. We are not prostrating as a supplicant asking some higher being for favor. We touch the Earth in order to realize the insight of interbeing, that we are a continuation of our ancestors.

After looking deeply into our spiritual ancestors and students and our blood ancestors, we visualize deeply our own children. We have children we like, who are close to being perfect. And we also have children with problems, who are far from perfect, who have made us suffer. Who are we not to accept our children as they are? When we accept them all as our children, we will feel deep peace. I do not have blood children, but I have many spiritual children. When I bend down to touch the Earth, I visualize them all.

Without roots, we cannot be happy. The practice must bring us back to our roots. So many people today are alienated from their cultures and traditions, and they suffer. I urge you to go back, to get re-rooted in your culture and tradition, using the insight of interbeing to generate the energy of wisdom and compassion. The First Prostration is for that.

### THE SECOND PROSTRATION

*Touching the Earth, I connect with all people and all species that are alive at this moment in this world with me. I am one with the wonderful pattern of life that radiates out in all directions. I see the close connection between myself and others, how we share happiness and suffering. I am one with those who were born disabled or who have become disabled because of war, accident, or illness. I am one with those who are caught in a situation of war or oppression. I am one with those who find no happiness in family life, who have no roots and no peace of mind, who are hungry for understanding and love, and who are looking for something beautiful, wholesome, and true to embrace and to believe in. I am someone at the point of death who is very afraid and does not know what is going to happen. I am a child who lives in a place where there is miserable poverty and disease, whose legs and arms are like sticks and who has no future. I am also the manufacturer of bombs that are sold to poor countries. I am the frog swimming in the pond and I am also the snake who needs the body of the frog to nourish its own body. I am the caterpillar or the ant that the bird is looking for to eat, but I am also the bird that is looking for the caterpillar or the ant. I am the forest that is being cut down. I am the rivers and the air that are being polluted and I am also the person who cuts down the*

*forest and pollutes the rivers and the air. I see myself in
all species and I see all species in me.*

I am one with all beings who are alive today—those great beings who have realized the truth of no-birth and no-death and are able to look at the forms of birth, death, joy, and suffering with calm eyes; those who have inner peace, love, and understanding and can touch that which is healing, nourishing, and refreshing and also have the capacity to embrace and act in the world with love and care; and those who are suffering because of physical or mental pain and anguish. I am someone who has enough peace, joy, and freedom to offer joy and non-fear to living beings. I see that I am not cut off. The love and happiness of great beings on this planet keep me from sinking in despair and help me to live my life in a meaningful way with true peace and happiness. I see all of them in me, and I see myself in all of them. The Second Prostration is represented by a horizontal line, the here and the now. When we touch the Earth in that position, we touch all living beings who are with us in this moment. We know that we are part of life, that life is seamless.

I wrote this poem in 1978 while I was trying to help boat people on the South China Sea:

*Do not say that I'll depart tomorrow—
even today I still arrive.*

*Look deeply: every second I am arriving
to be a bud on a Spring branch,
to be a tiny bird in my new nest,
to be a caterpillar in the heart of a flower,*

*to be a jewel hiding itself in a stone.*

*I still arrive, in order to laugh and to cry,*
*to fear and to hope.*
*The rhythm of my heart is the birth and death of all that is*
  *alive.*

*I am a mayfly metamorphosing*
*on the surface of the river.*
*And I am the bird*
*that swoops down to swallow the mayfly.*

*I am a frog swimming happily*
*in the clear water of a pond.*
*And I am the grass-snake*
*that silently feeds itself on the frog.*

*I am the child in Uganda, all skin and bones,*
*my legs as thin as bamboo sticks.*
*And I am the arms merchant,*
*selling deadly weapons to Uganda.*

*I am the twelve-year-old girl,*
*refugee on a small boat,*
*who throws herself into the ocean*
*after being raped by a sea pirate.*
*And I am the pirate,*
*my heart not yet capable*
*of seeing and loving.*

*I am a member of the politburo,*
*with plenty of power in my hands.*

*And I am the man who has to pay*
*his "debt of blood" to my people*
*dying slowly in a forced-labor camp.*

*My joy is like Spring, so warm*
*it makes flowers bloom all over the Earth.*
*My pain is like a river of tears,*
*so vast it fills the four oceans.*

*Please call me by my true names,*
*so I can hear all my cries and laughter at once,*
*so I can see that my joy and pain are one.*

*Please call me by my true names,*
*so I can wake up*
*and the door of my heart*
*could be left open,*
*the door of compassion.[1]*

We are all these people, but we are not drowned in the ocean of suffering, because we are capable of touching living beings who are capable of being peace, who bring relief and comfort to those who suffer. If we are mindful enough, we will touch these true bodhisattvas. Some of them are famous, but many just work silently, doing whatever they can to help. They are made of love, compassion, solidity, and freedom.

When I bow down to the Earth, I see myself in all those who are suffering, here and in the Third World. I see myself as a child in Uganda who has nothing to eat. I see a little

---

[1] Thich Nhat Hanh, *Call Me by My True Names*, p. 72 (see chap 6, n. 1).

child digging in the trash heap, hoping to find something he can exchange for food. I see men and women are in prison being tortured because they have protested against human rights abuses. I see myself as a young person who is caught by alcoholism and drugs, and as someone who has AIDS and little hope of a cure. I see myself as a young fanatic in a so-called religious sect who commits violent crimes out of anger and frustration. I see myself as a frog swimming happily in the clear water who is suddenly swallowed by a snake. I see myself as a rabbit running for my life, pursued by a panther. I suffer during these visualizations, but, at the same time, compassion is born in me.

Then I visualize myself as a person who has a very good heart, a bodhisattva with great love and compassion, working to help others. I see countless bodhisattvas working together, singing as they try to relieve the suffering of humans and other species on Earth. I participate in their joy, peace, and solidity; that is why I am not overwhelmed by feelings of despair or helplessness.

You might like to spend five or more minutes touching the Earth and visualizing and touching all these wonderful beings that inter-are with us in this very moment. We have to hold each other's hands and stand firm to preserve our solidity and freedom for the sake of the world. During the time we touch the Earth, we are aware of the presence of this worldwide Sangha, and we receive strength and energy from them. By calling their names or visualizing them, we can see our nature of interbeing with them. As we continue to touch them deeply, we are able to identify ourselves with *all* beings, in time (the First Prostration) and in space (the Second Prostration). If we succeed in doing this, we have already begun the Third Prostration.

## THE THIRD PROSTRATION

*Touching the Earth, I let go of my idea that I am this body and my life span is limited. I see that this body, made up of the four elements, is not really me and I am not limited by this body. I am part of a stream of life of spiritual and blood ancestors that for thousands of years has been flowing into the present and flows on for thousands of years into the future. I am one with my ancestors, I am one with all people and all species whether they are peaceful and fearless, or suffering and afraid. At this very moment I am present everywhere on this planet. I am also present in the past and in the future. The disintegration of this body does not touch me, just as when the plum blossom falls it does not mean the end of the plum tree. I see myself as a wave on the surface of the ocean, my nature is the ocean water. I see myself in all the other waves and all the other waves in me. The appearance and disappearance of the form of the wave does not affect the ocean. My Dharma body and wisdom life are not subject to birth and death. I see the presence of myself before my body manifested and after my body has disintegrated. Even in this moment, I see how I exist elsewhere than in this body. Seventy or eighty years is not my life span. My life span, like the life span of a leaf or of a Buddha, is limitless. I have gone beyond the idea that I am a body that is separated in space and time from all other forms of life.*

The Third Prostration is represented by a circle embracing the vertical and horizontal lines of the first two prostrations. This is the practice of the *Diamond Sutra*, removing the idea that this body is me and this life span is my life span. The first notion to be removed is the notion that I am only this body, and if this body is not here, I am not here. The Buddha repeated this teaching many times: "These eyes are not me. I am not caught in these eyes. I am life without boundaries. I have never been born. I will never die." So, please smile. Take my hands. We will be with each other always, in one form or another. That is the insight of interbeing, the insight of no-birth and no-death that you get when you practice the touching of the Buddha. It is the greatest relief. When we practice the Third Prostration, we touch deeply the world of no-birth and no-death, the world of nirvana here and now, the kingdom of God. "This body is not me. I am not caught in this body. I am life without boundaries." I am not caught in the ideas of being and nonbeing, birth and death. I fully recognize myself in all my ancestors and all my children, and in the trees and flowers that are standing in front of me.

One day, while I was breathing mindfully in front of a tree, I suddenly saw that I was able to breathe because of the tree. The tree and I mutually benefit from each other, and because of my mindfulness, I know how to protect the tree. Together, we belong to the stream of life. We inter-are. There is a tree in me, and there is a me in the tree. When you practice the Third Prostration, you realize that you are much more than your body, your feelings, your perceptions, your mental formations, and your consciousness. You are life without boundaries.

Whether you succeed in your practice of the Third Prostration depends on your practice of the First and the Second. During the First Prostration you realize that you are in a stream of being, along with your ancestors, your children, and their children. One morning on the Hawaiian island of Maui, I showed my friend Arnie Kotler the banana grove in the backyard of the Diamond Sangha. I pointed to a banana tree and told Arnie that this tree, after producing a flower and several bananas, will be cut down for another banana tree to have a place to grow. Arnie felt sad. He thought that when a banana tree comes down, it is the end of its life. I smiled and told him that if he knew what happened underneath in the soil, he wouldn't be sad. Beneath the surface there is a block of banana tree root where everything is one. If you cut down one tree, it is only to make room for another banana tree to grow. The banana trees are one; they are not independent of each other. In much the same way, you and your father, you and your mother, belong to the same reality. You do not have a separate self. They are in you and you are in them. During the First Prostration, you realize this and transcend the notion of an isolated self. If you succeed in the First Prostration, it is easy to remove the notion that this body is yourself.

During the Second Prostration, you visualize that you are the child in Uganda, the frog swallowed by the grass snake, and the bodhisattva who is singing and serving the people. If you succeed in this practice, it will be even easier to abandon the notion that your body is yourself. Your self is much larger. When I practice the Third Prostration, I remove the notion that this body is me and that these seventy years are my lifetime. The practice of the *Diamond Sutra* is to remove these four notions: self, person, living being, and life span.

If you practice looking deeply into the so-called self, you discover that it is made only of non-self elements. A flower is made only of non-flower elements—a seed, a cloud, the sun, minerals, and many other "non-flower elements." If you return all these non-flower elements back to their sources, the flower cannot be. That is why we can say that a self is made only of non-self elements.

The second notion that has to be removed is the notion of a person as a separate entity. We humans cannot be here without non-human elements, like animals, vegetables, and minerals. If we destroy the animals, vegetables, and minerals, we destroy ourselves as human beings. The *Diamond Sutra* is the most ancient text that teaches us to protect our environment, when it states that humans are made of non-human elements. If you destroy non-human elements, you destroy humans. Not only the notion of self as a separate entity has to be removed, but the notion of humans as an independent entity also has to be removed.

The third notion to be removed is the notion of living, animate beings. Looking deeply, we see that they are made of so-called inanimate substances like minerals and water. When you respect the rights of non-living beings, you respect the rights of living beings.

The last notion to be removed is life span. We believe that we begin to be at birth and cease to be after death. But if you practice looking deeply, you will see that you have infinite life, just like a Buddha. That is the teaching of the *Diamond Sutra.* We have to learn to put these teachings into practice in our daily lives. By practicing the Third Prostration every day, you will be able to remove the ideas of birth and death, self and life span, and you will no longer be afraid of death. You might think that the Third Prostration is more difficult to practice than the First or the Second, but the Third Prostration becomes easy when you succeed in the practice of the First and the Second Prostrations. We can free ourselves from the notions of birth and death and from the fear of dying by practicing the Three Prostrations. You will be of great help to those who are dying. You can inspire faith, confidence, and peace in them.

When you practice Touching the Earth, you are everywhere, not bound by birth or death, being or nonbeing. The great third-century Vietnamese Buddhist master Tang Hoi made it very clear that the exercises of mindful breathing proposed by the Buddha are to help us remove the notions, "I am this body," and "My life is confined by this period of time." When you touch the reality of no-birth and no-death, you transcend the idea that this body is you and the notion that this life span is you.

I practice the Three Prostrations every evening before sitting meditation. I light a stick of incense and enjoy watching the incense smoke rising. Then I practice the Three Prostrations. It takes about ten minutes. Then I go to the picture of my one hundred Angelinas, bow to them, and sit down for sitting meditation. The practice of the Three Prostrations can transform fear and anguish, restore your health, and reconcile yourself with your ancestors and your children. I recommend this practice highly. If you do it for one or two months, it can bring many benefits. Make the practice pleasant, so you enjoy doing it every day.

The Three Prostrations are a practice of insight. We transcend our personal self and see what is meant by "no-self," that we *are* our ancestors and our descendants. Use the above text of the Three Prostrations in the beginning, but after practicing for awhile, throw this text away and create your own version.

In three more years, we will arrive at the hill of the twenty-first century. I am advanced in years, and I don't know if I am going to arrive at the foot of that hill. But every day I think about my descendants who will climb it. In the year 2050, Brother Phâp Canh will be seventy-four years old. When he stands on top of that mountain, what will he see? He will look down and see the Sangha climbing up together. We cannot go up the hill of the twenty-first century as individuals. Our practice lies in doing it together.

My teacher's name was Thanh Quy. He died in 1968, after the Têt Offensive. But he is present today. He sent me on the path with all his love and care. Now I am carrying him, and I am transmitting him to you so you can carry him with you. If it were not for my teacher, how could I be here? We are just a stream called "life." The Sangha body of the Buddha is more than 2,500 years old. We may still be young, but we are also very old. Our Sangha is now all over the world, a little bit everywhere. Each part of the Sangha nourishes itself using different methods and different teachings, yet we are present in all these Sanghas, and our descendants will be present in them also. Our smile is also the smile of others. Our suffering is the suffering of others. To see this is the realization of no-self. We need this insight to be able to take firm steps on the path of life.

If you think you are alone, that is an illusion. You can touch the elements of happiness that are already here and be peace in the present moment. It depends on your way of looking. Please learn and practice the art of mindful living, the art of being happy and bringing happiness to others. This is love meditation. This is living deeply in the present moment. We rely on you to do it.